School Re Behavio.

Children Who Can't or Won't Go To School

George B. Haarman, Psy.D., LMFT

Foundations: Education and Consultation Press
Louisville, Kentucky

First published in the United States in 2012 by
Foundations:Education and Consultation

FOR INFORMATION ADDRESS:
Foundations: Education and Consultation
1400 Browns Lane
Louisville, Kentucky 40207

ISBN:978-0-615-70847-8

For my wife, my daughters, and my granddaughters

School Refusal Behavior: Children Who Can't or Won't Go To School

Table of Contents

Chapter One
Truancy versus School Refusal

When the first organized school opened its doors, it was likely that there was a child who failed to attend. Failure to attend school is a problem that has existed for as long as there have been organized schools. Early literature labeled these children as **truant** derived from the French word "truand" meaning beggar, parasite, lazy person, naughty child, or rogue. However, in addition to those children who refused to attend school in an antisocial fashion, there was a gradual recognition of a subset of children who were absent from school who did not fit the typical patterns or dynamics of a truant. For this subset of children, their absences were more emotionally based than oppositional. In an early definition of anxiety based absenteeism, Broadwin (1932) defined some children as exhibiting a set of behaviors in refusing school that "are an attempt to obtain love, or escape from real situations to which it is difficult to adjust." Eventually, this group of children was identified as school phobic and their absence from school was identified as *School Phobia.*

School phobia was identified in the 1940's as a psychoneurotic disorder characterized by overlapping phobic and obsessive tendencies (Johnson et al., 1941). School phobia was identified as fear-based school non-attendance in response to a specific stimuli or situation that was a part of attending school. In many cases it also involved separation anxiety, which was present before the advent of attending school, and was comorbid with generalized anxiety, somatic complaints, depression, and family conflict. Early thinking identified three essential elements of school phobia: 1) acute child anxiety with hypochondriacal and compulsive elements resulting from a wish for dependence, 2) increased anxiety in the child's mother (primary caretaker) as a result of some identifiable stressor, and 3) a historically unresolved, overdependent mother child relationship and regression to a period of mutual satisfaction. An alternative, less clinical term, **school refusal behavior**, was later used in Great Brittan to define similar problems in children who did not attend school because of emotional distress, but who did not appear to be pathological in other respects. The term school phobia was felt to be overly clinical and psychopathological and the term school refusal was adopted as a broader encompassing term.

One difficulty with the professional literature, which has lead to some confusion, is the wide variety of terminology associated with this phenomenon and how the terminology has been used imprecisely. Kearney (2008b) attempted to provide some clarification and precision with definitions of specific terminology. *Absenteeism* is defined as a legitimate or illegitimate absence from school or class. He estimates that 80 percent of the children absent from school are absent for legitimate reasons and that the remaining 20 percent are *school refusers*, defined as, the child who does not fully attend school and has no reasonable or justifiable circumstances for the absence. This illegitimate absenteeism may be child-motivated or parent motivated, i.e. requiring the child to stay home to babysit younger siblings or care for an elderly grandparent. Parent-motivated absenteeism is often referred to as *school withdrawal.*

A child-motivated absence is referred to by a variety of terms, contributing to some of the confusion, including: *truancy, school refusal, school phobia, or "dropping out."* *Truancy* has different meanings, including a legal definition, which may vary from jurisdiction to jurisdiction. It generally refers to an illegal or illegitimate absence from school or an unexcused absence without parental permission. *School Refusal* generally refers to anxiety based absenteeism. These children have difficulty going to or remaining in school and are often described as fearful, anxious, sad, timid, and shy. However, significant overlap exists between youth traditionally described as truant and those labeled as school refusers. Many youth who refuse school show a combination of anxiety based and acting out behavior.

School refusal is sometimes linked to more specific concepts such as *school phobia, separation anxiety, and dropping out. School phobia* refers to fear based absenteeism, as when a child is specifically afraid of something related to school attendance, such as, a bully, an animal in the classroom, the lunch room, or the bus ride. The term *school phobia* is used less frequently in the professional literature and Kearney (2008b) has advocated "it is best to avoid using this term when consulting with fellow professionals and parents." *Separation anxiety* refers to the difficulty of the child, and sometimes the parent, to separate in key situations such as going to school or staying with a babysitter. Fear and separation anxiety are often components of school refusal. *School dropouts or dropping out* refers to premature and permanent departure from school prior to graduation. According to the National Center for Education Statistics (2006), the dropout rate for 16-24 year olds in the United States is 10.3 percent.

Kearney (2008a) has suggested that the most appropriate terminology is one which deals with all youth with problematic absenteeism under one rubric called *school refusal behavior* and to identify these youth as *school refusers. School refusal behavior* refers to child-motivated refusal to attend school or difficulties with remaining in class the entire day. The

6

term *school refusal behavior* refers to a collection of behaviors along a continuum ranging from the child who attends school but is under duress and pleads for non-attendance to a child who is completely absent from school for an extended period of time.

A review of the literature would reveal that there appear to be two very different dynamics and characteristics which differentiate the typical truant from a school refuser (Kearney, 2008b). This dynamic can be readily seen in the following chart which illustrates the distinctions between those children who are school refusers versus those individuals who operate out of a truancy dynamic:

Behavioral Characteristics of School Refusers and Truants	
School Refusal	*Truancy*
Severe emotional stress about attending school: may include anxiety, temper tantrums, depression, or somatic issues	Lack of excessive anxiety or fear about attending school
Parents are aware of absence or the child convinces parents to allow him to stay at home	Children often attempt to conceal their absence from parents
Absence of significant behavioral or antisocial problems	Frequent antisocial behavior, often in the company of antisocial peers
During school hours, the child stays home because it is safe	During school hours, the child is somewhere other than home
A willingness to do homework and complies by completing work at home	Lack of willingness to do schoolwork or meet academic expectations

School Refusal (Kearney, 2001) is "child motivated refusal to attend school or difficulties remaining in school for an entire day." Berg (1996) defined school refusal as severe difficulty attending school often resulting in a prolonged absence; severe emotional upset when faced with the prospect of attending school; staying at home with the parents' knowledge; and an absence of anti social characteristics. School refusal would not include absences as a result of chronic physical illnesses, absences motivated by parents, homelessness, chronic runaways, or non child initiated absences. Berg (1997) further expanded the concept as a condition characterized by reluctance or refusal to go to school by a child who: 1) seeks the comfort and security of home, preferring to remain close to parental figures; 2) displays evidence of emotional upset or unexplained physical symptoms at the prospect of going to school; 3) manifests no severe antisocial tendencies; and 4) does not attempt to conceal the problem from parents. King and Bernstein et al.(2001) expanded the concept to include difficulty attending school associated with emotional distress, especially anxiety and depression.

Kearney and Silverman (1996) further expanded the definition of school refusal to include those children who have difficulty remaining in school for the entire day. They identify school refusal as a continuum of behaviors, which includes consistently missing school all the way to rarely missing school, but attending under extreme duress.

School refusal includes those who :
1) are completely absent from school
2) initially attend and then leave during the school day
3) may attend for all or part of the day, but only after a behavioral incident at home or on the way to school (tantrum, vomiting, etc.)
4) and, those children who display unusual distress during the school day and plead for nonattendance or create excuses to go home.

In addition, school refusal is often viewed on a continuum of severity and chronicity. Many children will experience a brief period in their life where attending school is particularly difficult or emotionally overwhelming. For many youth, this is a brief condition that spontaneously resolves itself after a few days. For others, once the problematic behavior appears, it becomes self-reinforcing and will persist for long periods of time without significant intervention. Kearney and Silverman (1996), Silverman and Kurtines (1996), and Kearney (2001) identified three levels of severity of school refusal:

Self-corrective school refusal refers to children whose initial absenteeism remits spontaneously within a two week period.

Acute school refusal behavior refers to children whose absenteeism lasts from 2 weeks to one calendar year.

Chronic school refusal behavior refers to children whose absenteeism lasts longer than one calendar year and overlaps two school years.

This identification of school refusal related to the degree of severity and chronicity was further expanded by Setzer and Salhauer (2001) when they outlined the varying types of school refusal behavior:

Initial School Refusal Behavior – lasts for a brief period (less than two weeks) and may resolve without intervention

Substantial School Refusal Behavior – occurs a minimum of two weeks and requires some form of intervention

Acute School Refusal Behavior – two weeks to one year, being a consistent problem for a majority of the time

Chronic School Refusal Behavior – interferes with, or overlaps, two or more academic years

Chapter Two

Characteristics of School Refusers

Children present with many different reasons for refusing to attend school. In many instances Separation Anxiety Disorder or a history of separation in the past may create an underlying anxiety about being away from home or parental figures, which school attendance requires. Many children in the foster care system have experienced significant anxiety as a result of the physical and emotional separations which typically occur. These separations create an underlying anxiety which makes attending school extremely difficult.

Other children who become anxious about attending school may be struggling with the fear of losing a parent through illness, divorce, or death. In many instances the school refusal may actually begin after the parent recovers from an illness in which the child remained at home rather than attend school. The absence continues despite the lack of a threat from the parent's illness. These children may engage in magical thinking or create disaster scenarios, in which something bad will happen to a parent if they are not there to monitor or prevent the disaster. Fear of physical and emotional abandonment may make it difficult for the child to have his or her parents out of their sight and out of their "control." Many of these children who refuse school may have experienced an unstable family situation where frequent physical moves and family changes have occurred. This creates an underlying anxiety about not being able to control the home situation while they are at school.

Changes in the stability of the system at home and in the family, such as frequent deaths in the family, divorce, moves to a new house, separations, transfers to another job or community, or jealousy of new siblings, can all cause a family system to be so unstable that a generalized state of anxiety may result. This instability can be managed or contained by a reluctance or refusal to attend school. A family system where parents are overly anxious themselves may actually transmit unspoken messages to the child about attending school. The child may view the anxiety of the parents as being caused by their attendance at school and may feel it is their fault that the parent is anxious about the child attending school. The youth may feel that they are obligated to "take care of" the anxious parent by refusing to attend school, thereby making the parent feel more comfortable and secure.

The root anxiety, which the school refuser is experiencing in a school situation, may vary significantly according to age (King and Bernstein, 2001). Younger children may be more anxious about being separated from caregivers, fear a teacher, become anxious about riding the bus, or fear being picked on by older children. Frequently middle/high school refusers have concerns about academic performance, worries about making friends, eating in the cafeteria, using the school bathroom, changing for gym, being called on for class, or being made fun of or ostracized by peers. For some children there are legitimate fears of being bullied, gangs, school violence, or being ostracized and ridiculed.

Behavioral symptoms are also variable in their presentation, but for many children they may include fearfulness, panic, crying, temper tantrums, threats of self-harm, and somatic complaints. Many children who are school refusers may utilize a variety of verbal or even physical protests each morning before school. Their disruptive behaviors may be a

12

"proactive" attempt to avoid going to school. By being so disruptive or behaviorally out of control, the child hopes that parents may acquiesce and allow the child to stay at home. These behaviors may be openly defiant, excessively disruptive, and may escalate to clearly unacceptable behaviors as a desperation move to avoid school attendance. For some school refusers, their behavior may be more passive as evidenced by lethargy, delays, stalling, or may take on a more "passive aggressive" quality as evidenced by the child who "misses the bus" or who is chronically late due to "oversleeping."

One strategy employed by many school refusers to avoid attending school is to have physical illnesses or bodily symptoms. These symptoms may be factitious in nature or may truly be experienced as psychosomatic correlates of their emotional or psychological discomfort. School refusers frequently have a large number of physical symptoms including autonomic, gastrointestinal, and muscular symptoms. Dizziness, headaches, trembling, heart palpitations, chest pains, abdominal pain, nausea, vomiting, diarrhea, back pain, and joint pain without any organic basis are frequently experienced by school refusers. In some situations school refusers may experience symptoms, which are contradictory in nature or cannot exists simultaneously, involving both the parasympathetic and sympathetic nervous systems.

The school refusal behaviors may be a part of an identifiable family interaction pattern, and a variety of family characteristics have been identified as associated with school refusers (Kearney & Silverman, 1995). One of the more obvious dynamics is the existence of overdependence between parent and child. This lack of autonomy on the part of the child or unwillingness of the parent to allow for independent functioning may produce significant anxiety due to the fact that the act of attending school calls for separation and autonomous

13

functioning. The youngest child in the family is particularly vulnerable to school refusal, probably as a result of over dependency or enmeshment issues (Kearney and Silverman, 2002). The opposite extreme is also seen in families of school refusers, whose families display extreme detachment. These children often feel vulnerable and lacking in support to deal with the challenges of attending school. Many children who struggle with attending school come out of families where physical and social isolation is common. For these children, the social aspects of attending school are often overwhelming and escape behavior may ensue. A number of other family dynamics have been identified as highly correlated with school refusal, including overprotective parents, anxious mothers and ineffective fathers, and high levels of marital tension.

Kearney and Silverman (1995) identified six types of families of school refusers: 1) enmeshed, 2) conflicted, 3) detached, 4) isolated, 5) mixed, and 6) healthy.

Enmeshed Family -The dominant aspect of these families is an apparent lack of boundaries and individual dynamics which prevent boundaries from being recognized or honored. Parents in these situations are characterized as overprotective and cannot tolerate their child experiencing any difficulty or discomfort. These parents respond too quickly and disproportionately to any unpleasant situation that the child may experience at school rather than allow the youth to work through their own difficulties. An individual parent or both parents in the enmeshed family may be overindulgent, not setting any limitations on behavior and allowing the child too much decision making authority. The child may exhibit symptoms that serve the dual purpose of avoiding school attendance and at the same time eliciting a strong nurturing and pampering response from parents. Enmeshed families have a strong need to insure that children remain dependent and any attempt at developing

14

autonomy and self-sufficiency are overtly or covertly discouraged.

Conflicted Families- In many families, the level of hostility, violence, and conflict often threatens the stability of the family. These families are constantly in conflict and in many instances violence, threats, and coercion are the forces which maintain the connections between family members. School refusal and the school refusing child can serve as a distraction to insure that the level of conflict does not reach critical mass and threaten the existence of the family. A child with school attendance issues in some situations becomes the "lightning rod" for the family conflict. Having a family member absorb the family conflict leaves the family at a systemic state of stability which does not threaten the dynamic of the family. The level of conflict often keeps the system under constant threat, in chaos, and full of uncertainty. This family "background noise" creates anxiety in all family members and for the school refusing child, this heightened state of constant anxiety may make adapting to the normal stresses of school attendance overwhelming and unbearable.

Detached Families – Many school refusers exist within a family environment with little real interpersonal connection between members. These youth are raised in a home with one or both parents physically or emotionally absent and the school refuser may have very little sense that the adults in their life will be there for them, if needed. Increasingly, children are being raised by other relatives or as a part of the foster care system and have limited emotional connection to their "family" of caretakers. In these situations there is often little involvement among members and many youth are left with the feeling that no one "has my back" or will come to my assistance in dealing with the problems which I might be experiencing at school.

Isolated Families – Children who live in rural or isolated settings may experience a great deal of difficulty in adjusting to school attendance. For many of these children they have had little contact with individuals who were not family members or a part of their small group of friends and neighbors. Exposure to a new and unfamiliar setting and new and unfamiliar people can be quite anxiety producing. Having to adapt to and interact with youth and school personnel who come from a different socioeconomic status, culture, or who have different value systems can be a threatening experience. Even children who live in metropolitan areas may feel a social isolation if their family has limited contact with the larger community. Increasing their level of social interaction, when they have had limited opportunities to develop or practice these skills outside the family, may make them struggle socially, which leads to further social isolation.

Healthy Families – To automatically assume that a child who is refusing to attend school must come from a dysfunctional family would be a mistake. Many school refusers come from very healthy and functional family situations, but may have difficulty attending school due to a specific situation like a punitive teacher, a bully, or other stressors. Children who struggle academically may also be school refusers, since they find little reward or reinforcement in attending school, despite parental encouragement and support.

Mixed Traits – For some school refusers, their families may display two or more traits that are associated with school refusal. Enmeshed families are often also highly conflictual due to a lack of honoring and respecting appropriate boundaries. Many isolated families also display a high degree of detachment within individual family members.

16

Demographic Characteristics of School Refusers

According to the U.S. National Center of Education Statistics (2006), 5.5 percent of students are absent on a typical school day. In a typical month, 19% of fourth graders and 20% of eighth graders missed at least three days of school; 7% of fourth graders and 7% of eighth graders missed more than five days in a month. Rates are higher in inner city schools as compared to rural schools, higher among schools where a majority of students are eligible for the free lunch program, higher in public schools as compared to private schools, greater in high schools than middle and elementary schools, and more prominent in large schools as compared to smaller schools. Duckworth and DeJung (1989) have estimated that the rate of youth absent without a valid excuse is about 4 percent. They also estimate that 5 percent to 10 percent of all school children are late in the morning or miss part of the day and that 6 percent to 10 percent of those attending school are attending under identifiable anxiety based duress.

A "best guess" is that 5% to 28% of children display some aspect of school refusal behavior at some point in their life (Kearney, 2007b). Kearney also estimated that for any given day, 2-5% of enrolled children are school refusers. School absenteeism and school refusal prevalence rates rival those of major childhood behaviors disorders, such as depression, substance abuse, oppositional defiant disorder, and attention deficit hyperactivity disorder (Costello, Eger, and Angold, 2005). King and Bernstein (2001) reported that school refusal is equally common among boys and girls, but female school refusal may be more fear based, while male school refusers may be more oppositional based. Ollendick & Mayer (1984) indicated that school refusal can occur at all ages, but peaks at 5-7, 11, and 14 (kindergarten, 6th grade, and 9th grade). Periods of transition, such as attending a new school, moves to a new home, new brother or sister, or a sick parent, often increase the likelihood of school refusal (Kearney & Albano, 2007). No socioeconomic or gender differences are noted. There also does not appear to be a relationship to academic or intellectual ability, although prolonged school refusal will eventually impact academic achievement (Egger, Costello, & Angold, 2003). Kearney and Albano (2007) reported that generally children age 5 to 11 tend to refuse school to avoid negative affect and/or to receive attention, while youth 12 to 17 tend to refuse school to escape aversive social or evaluative situations or to gain tangible rewards.

Long-term Sequelae

While school refusal is often minimized as "a phase," a stage of development, or a normal rite of passage, it would appear that in many situations school refusal is a predictor of more lasting issues which may persist into adulthood (King, Ollendick, & Tonge, 1995). While school refusal may not be causative of adult problems, in many situations school refusal, which is not addressed emphatically, is predictive of later problems. A review of the literature (Kearney, 2008b) indicated a number of studies indicating a relationship between school refusal and academic underachievement, dropout rate, increased psychiatric care, and autonomy issues. A reluctance to physically leave the family of origin, difficulty emotionally leaving the family of origin, and delinquency and criminal offenses have been correlated with early school refusal (Bernstein et al., 2001 and Flakierska-Praquin et al., 1997). Kogan et al. (2005) found that early absenteeism is associated with school dropout, an event which leads to a disconnection from school based health programs, economic deprivation, and marital, social, and psychiatric problems in adulthood.

School refusers would also seem to be at risk for developing substance abuse issues. Chou et al. (2006) and Halfors et al. (2006) have demonstrated a correlation between alcohol abuse, school absenteeism, and school refusal behaviors. Roebuck, French, and Hurrelmann (1999) have also established a correlation between school refusal and early marijuana use.

Internalizing versus Externalizing

School refusers tend to display behavior that is school avoidant utilizing an internalizing/externalizing continuum. For some children, school refusal is a way of internalizing aspects of their environment, which make them feel uncomfortable or fearful. Fears (specific phobias), anxiety, somatic complaints, depression, and general negative affectivity are frequently experienced by the school refuser. Somatic complaints are frequently reported by school refusers. Freemont (2003) indicated that 56 percent of school refusers sampled displayed a primary diagnosis of anxiety disorders, including Generalized Anxiety Disorder (36.5 %), Separation Anxiety (27.0 %), Social Phobia (33.6%), and Other Anxiety Disorders (PTSD, OCD, Agoraphobia, etc). They also noted that approximately 66% of all school refusing youth presented with some somatic complaints.

Other school refusers tend to externalize symptoms through a number of "acting out" behaviors including a variety of physical, verbal, passive/aggressive behaviors, and temper tantrums. These are assumed to be triggered by internal psychological factors. These behavioral issues can take a

19

number of forms and serve a number of purposes. Many behaviors may "advertise" the nature of the anxiety such as clinging to a parent, or being physically aggressive toward a teacher or other students. Externalizing behaviors such as hiding, repeating the same question or statement, constant talking, or making excessive demands may be a method of avoiding or ameliorating an anxiety provoking situation. Tantrums, suicide threats, threats of self-harm, or threats of harm to others obtain attention from parents, school personnel, and others. A variety of classroom misbehaviors may be attempts to escape the school setting or force parent contact for reassurance. For many school refusers, their disruptive behaviors may be a test of parental resolve or a manipulation for concrete rewards (bribes, bargaining, or rewards after initial non-compliance). Behaviors may include verbal or physical threats to intimidate parents into acquiescence or to rescue the child from the school situation.

Continuum of School Refusal Behavior

As a group, school refusers are not defined or described in a particularly meaningful way through a single category or description (Freemont, 2003). School refusal behavior covers a wide spectrum on a continuum. This classification includes those who attend school, but are under extreme psychological duress and stress, those who display repeated misbehavior in the mornings to avoid school, children who are chronically late for school, those with episodic or repeated absences, and those who are completely absent for long periods of time. These children and their behaviors may share little in common other than a motivation to avoid attending

20

school. The refusal or avoidance of school is often the only common characteristic.

Kearney (2008b) has stated that, as a group, school refusers are non-homogeneous and the classification or designation as a "school refuser" is rendered almost meaningless due to the broad spectrum of behaviors and motivations. Any attempt to intervene with these children in a "one size fits all" approach is likely to be doomed from the start. The behaviors themselves, the underlying causes, and the factors that reinforce school refusal behavior vary widely from individual to individual. The variability calls for an approach different from traditional approaches to behavioral change.

Most behavioral difficulties are traditionally approached from a categorical model geared toward separating phenomena (observed behavior) into discrete categories. This is the underlying basis of the Medical Model and the basis for the *Diagnostic and Statistical Manual of Mental Disorders –TR-IV (2000).* Albano et al., (2003) indicated that the *DSM* system represents the categorical classification approach, attempting to separate disorders into clinically derived and mutually exclusive classes based upon a hierarchical model. The categorical approach as espoused by Kennedy, (1965) and Coolidge et al., (1957) assumed that school refusal behavior can be viewed as relatively separate phenomena. At the core are symptoms that distinguish the presence or absence of a disorder. Unfortunately, the enormous variability in school refusers makes it difficult to derive any meaningful categories or symptoms that reflect the complexity of the phenomenon. A categorical approach to school refusal does allow us to attempt to develop descriptors of the behavior and thereby differentiate between those who meet criteria for school refusal and those who do not, but these differentiations are not particularly meaningful. A categorical approach to school refusal also runs the risk of inappropriately classifying or diagnosing an individual as a "school refuser" when there may be more significant issues existing. Also a categorical approach runs the risk of the negative labeling which so often occurs once someone has been identified as "abnormal" or as differing from the population as a whole. Many times this negative labeling can lead to inappropriate functioning or a self-fulfilling prophesy.

Another typical approach for dealing with individuals whose behavior is outside the norm, which attempts to avoid the negative aspects of a categorical model, is a dimensional approach. Dimensional models such as Achenbach (1991) viewed behavior on a continuum and are only concerned with behaviors that create dysfunction or a lack of appropriate adaptation. Behavior is viewed on a continuum from adaptive to dysfunctional or from absent to severe. Unfortunately with school refusal, delineating behavior on a continuum does not particularly provide any insight as to the nature of the phenomenon or lead to reasonable interventions.

A more appropriate model for working with individuals who are school refusers might be to view the school refusal behavior through a Functional Model. A Functional Model looks at the purpose the behavior serves and what motivates the behavior or what maintains the behavior. (Kearney, 2001 and Kearney and Albano, 2007)

Chapter Three

A Functional Model of School Refusal Behavior (Kearney, 2001 and Kearney & Albano, 2000 & 2007)

All human behavior is purposeful. By understanding the function or purpose of a child's school refusal, we can increase the likelihood of effectively intervening. In addition, all behavior which is not reinforced extinguishes over time. For school refusal, understanding the underlying factors which maintain or reinforce the behavior will be a key in making the therapeutic changes necessary for an effective intervention. Kearney and Albano (2007) advocated a functional analysis of the problem behaviors on both a descriptive level (soliciting information from the child and parents through interviewing and rating scales) and an experimental level (involving direct observation of the school refusal behavior). This analysis can form a synthesis to determine which intervention approaches are most likely to be successful. While school refusal behavior may take many different forms or varying degrees of severity, the functions or reasons behind the behaviors are relatively few and can be grouped as either an attempt to avoid negative experiences associated with school or to pursue positive experiences by not attending school.

Avoidance of Negative Experiences
1. Avoidance of Stimuli that Provoke a Sense of General Negative Affect
2. Escape from Aversive Social or Evaluative Situations

Pursuit of Positive Experiences
1. Attention Seeking Behaviors
2. Tangible Reinforcement Outside the School

Children who are refusing school to avoid negative experiences may be attempting to avoid a particular stimuli or series of stimuli related to school attendance that ultimately result in a negative experience. The stimuli to be avoided may be something specific like a bully, or more pervasive like the structure and discipline of the school setting. Other school refusers may be attempting to escape from the negative social or evaluative aspects of attending school. Some school refusing children may be pursuing a positive experience through refusing school such as tangible reinforcers like staying at home, attention, or more desirable activities. Kearney (2007a) speculated that as many as a third of the children may refuse school for multiple functions or purposes. For example some children may initially refuse school to avoid the negative experience of an overly punitive teacher. If they are successful in remaining at home, they may realize the desirability of remaining at home and then refuse school for both positive experiences and avoidance of negative experiences. Children who refuse school for multiple reasons may require a more sophisticated intervention strategy combining multiple approaches.

The Functional Model of school refusal recognizes these fundamental distinctions and approaches change in behavior on the basis of these different purposes and motivations. Dube and Orpinas (2009) found that in a sample of upper elementary school refusers, 17.2 percent had a multiple profile which included elements of several purposes and 60.6 percent were refusing to attend school from a primary motivation of attention seeking.

Relevant research validating the approach of a Functional Model includes uncontrolled work as well as controlled studies of prescriptive and non-prescriptive treatment (Chorpita et al., 1996; Kearney, 2002a; Kearney, Pursell, & Alvarez, 2001; Kearney & Silverman, 1990, 1999). Recent data supports the use of a Functional Model of school refusal behavior. Among a sample of 222 youths with school refusal behaviors, Kearney (2007b) demonstrated that utilizing structural modeling to identify the function of school refusal was a better predictor of school absenteeism than traditional measures of fear, anxiety, and depression.

Silverman et al. (2008) concluded that sufficient information is available to include this form of prescriptive treatment as fitting the criteria as a *Possibly Efficacious Treatment Approach* for school refusal. To gain a fuller understanding of the different functions which school refusal might serve, each of the four functions will be reviewed in detail.

Function 1: School Refusal for Avoidance of Stimuli That Provoke a Sense of General Negative Affect (SPNA)

For many school refusers, specific stimuli or situations (bus ride, lunchroom, fire alarm, animal in classroom, restrooms, etc.) produce negative or uncomfortable feelings about school which the child feels he or she must avoid. Some children may not be able to identify the specific fear-related stimuli. This may not be resistance, but is due to a lack of specificity or an inability to conceptualize and verbalize what is making them uncomfortable about school. What they are very clear about is they "don't want to be at school" and that "being at school makes me feel yucky." Kearney (2008a) has indicated that the child's distress about attending school has multiple components including a physical component, cognitive component, and behavioral component. The physical component may include shakiness, nausea, headaches, and muscle pain, etc. The distress or general negative affect also contains a cognitive or thinking component which may create ongoing questioning or self-statements about going to school or verbal pleas regarding school attendance. A behavioral component may include overt symptoms such as crying, tantrums, withdrawal, distractibility, and irritability.

Many of the children in this grouping (SPNA), score higher on measures of general anxiety and on symptoms of depression. These children do not display problematic behaviors otherwise and tend to be lower on attention problems, delinquency, or aggressive behaviors. They characteristically tend to be more dependent than their peers. Typically, these children have few other emotional issues and come from generally healthy families. Diagnostically, these children are characterized as having Generalized Anxiety Disorder (GAD), Depression/Dysthymia, Separation Anxiety Disorder, Social Phobia, and Specific Phobias. In addition, this group engages in significant somatization as an attempt to avoid the negative stimuli associated with school (Kearney, 2001).

Function 2: School Refusal to Escape from Aversive Social or Evaluative Situations (EASE)

For another group of school refusers, school is a particularly negative and punitive experience due to the social or the evaluative aspects of the school setting. For these individuals, school is the place in their life where they experience significant embarrassment, shame, ridicule, rejection, debasement, and even abuse from their peers or from school personnel. These school refusers may literally lack the capacity for measuring up to the expectations for academic progress and learning and are constantly receiving "a negative evaluation." For this group, school is the place where they are constantly reminded that they are not good enough, smart enough, quick enough, and talented enough to achieve at a normal level, let alone, excel. Many of these school refusers (EASE), struggle with common situations, which naturally occur, in the social and evaluative setting we call public education. Common examples of *social situations,* which are difficult for these youth, might include interactions with peers in the hallways, "free form" or unstructured situations, attending assemblies, group work, talking in class, extracurricular activities, starting or maintaining conversations, or working on projects with other students. Common performance situations that these youth may struggle with could include speaking before class, writing on the board, being called on in class, tests or graded situations, performance classes (i.e. physical education, music, etc.), eating publicly, or taking tests and receiving graded results.

For these youth (EASE), school refusal might be motivated by a desire to avoid certain people (teachers or peers) due to past embarrassment, shame, or ridicule. This type of school refuser may typically be a child who struggles to perform up to expectations or who has real difficulty fitting in with the other children. Kearney and Albano (2000) reported that this particular group of school refusers may have higher scores on measures of general anxiety, score higher on symptoms of depression, experience higher levels of social anxiety, and display significant levels of withdrawal and somatization. Many of these school refusers come out of situations and settings of physical or social isolation. They may also experience significant family and community detachment. This lack of a social experience base makes interacting with others in a school setting particularly troublesome, awkward, and difficult. The lack of experience leads to poor social interactions and greater anxiety about the social aspects of school.

Kearney (2008a) has identified that these youth (EASE) tend to be somewhat older (11-17) than those who avoid school to avoid a negative affect (SPNA). Cognitively they are more mature and can point to specific situations which cause their distress. This social and evaluative anxiety overlaps with the natural egocentrism of adolescence and when intensified may result in school refusal behaviors. These youth may "skip" particular classes, ask for frequent schedule changes, avoid entering the building until the last minute to limit social contact, shy away from speaking to classmates or teachers, or completely stay away from situations where large numbers of students are present. Diagnostically these youth are frequently classified as having Generalized Anxiety Disorder (GAD), Social Phobia, Depression/Dysthymia, or a premorbid Avoidant Personality Disorder (Kearney, 2005).

28

Function 3: School Refusal for Attention Seeking Behavior (ASB)

For some school refusers, their behavior is motivated by a desire to gain something positive rather than avoiding a negative that comes with attendance. They may be seeking positive rewards for non-attendance, including intangibles such as attention or sympathy. The child seeking attention may have little distress about school related items or situations. In fact, they often attend school easily and smoothly as long as a parent or older sibling is allowed to attend with them. If the parent or sibling is not allowed to attend, their behavior is usually geared toward going home or going to a parent's workplace.

Kearney and Albano (2007) reported that the in-school behavior of these youths (ASB) includes noncompliance, defiance, tantrums, manipulations, or oppositional behaviors. These behaviors may not be limited to school, but may be displayed in a proactive fashion at home to avoid separation and prevent going to school. The attention seeking school refuser may engage in various morning misbehaviors to avoid school and stay at home, while simultaneously increasing the likelihood of attention (tantrums, clinging, locking themselves in their room, exaggerated physical symptoms, noncompliance, running away, etc.). On some level they (ASB) understand that not going to school assists them in obtaining the positive experience of attention and staying at home. In order to get the attention and sympathy, which necessarily comes with their refusal to attend school, these youth may exaggerate physical or emotional symptoms. Complaints may include a variety of vague physical symptoms such as headaches, stomachaches, back pain, etc. for which no organic basis can be found. Some may even go to the extent of "playing dead" as a method of avoiding school attendance.

The attendance patterns of these youth (ASB) may show a great number of "tardies," frequent requests to go home early, frequent time spent in the nurse's office, or badgering teachers to let them go home. While many of these youth (ASB) experience comorbid separation anxiety, not all youth whose behavior serves this function have significant issues with separation anxiety. In a larger sense their behavior may be more manipulative to obtain parental or school personnel attention. Many youth who naturally experience some degree of separation anxiety about going to school may exaggerate this discomfort to manipulate, control, or solicit attention. Kearney (2001) reported that for this group, "separation anxiety" may need to be viewed as one of three types:

1. Children who are truly anxious when separated from caregivers
2. Children who are more broadly seeking general attention
3. Children who are both anxious about separation and also seeking attention

These school refusers (ASB) tend to be younger (mean age 9.6) and are from families with very low levels of independence and autonomous functioning (enmeshed). Frequently, there is a long history of acquiescence to the child's wishes or demands that has been achieved through emotional terrorism or manipulation on the child's part. Diagnostically these school refusers tend to struggle with Separation Anxiety Disorder, Generalized Anxiety Disorder (GAD), and Oppositional Defiant Disorder (Kearney, 2001)

Function 4: School Refusal for Tangible Reinforcers Outside of School (TROS)

For another group of school refusers, the function that their school refusal behavior serves is to allow them to pursue positive experiences. By not going to school, these youth may be pursuing a variety of tangible reinforcers which they can only attain by not going to school. Often the refusal is an attempt to pursue reinforcers, which are particularly pleasing and powerful, such as sleeping, TV, video games, internet, friends, day parties, the mall, etc. For these youth (TROS), their school refusal is less anxiety based and more a result of impulsivity or an inability to delay gratification. Their school refusal may be evolving into a more truant dynamic with very little distress about attending school, but distress about not attaining a rewarding experience (Kearney, 2001).

Typically these youth (TROS) have lower levels of anxiety, depression, or distress about going to school. "I could go to school; no big deal; but I'm not; and you can't make me." These youth are generally older and display more attention problems, delinquent behaviors, and aggressiveness. Families are more conflicted and have low levels of cohesion. Communication between parent and child is typically non-functional or non-existent. Diagnostically, these youth experience Generalized Anxiety Disorder (GAD), Oppositional Defiant Disorder, Conduct Disorder, and Depression/Dysthymia (Kearney and Albano, 2007).

Function 5: Multiple Functions

In some situations, a youth's school refusal behavior may simultaneously serve one or more functions. Kearney and Albano (2007) reported that "some children, perhaps as many as a third, refuse school for two or more functions." In other circumstances, the purpose or function of the original school refusal behaviors can morph over time to serve a different purpose or function. A common example is a child who is so distressed about stimuli at school, which produces a negative affect, that he begs his parents to let him remain at home (SPNA). Once at home, a secondary positive experience of parental attention (ASB) or the possibility of pursuing tangible rewards (TROS), internet, TV, special meals, etc. may take over as the primary motivation and ultimately become the purpose of the refusal to attend school. Another example might be the child who has been out of school for a long period of time due to attention seeking behaviors (ASB), and then becomes anxious and overwhelmed at the prospect of having to return to a great deal of make-up work or to have to interact with new teachers and peers. Youth who refuse school for multiple reasons or functions are likely to require a more complex intervention. Likewise, youth who have missed school for a longer period of time will require a more complex intervention than a child who has just started to refuse school.

Chapter Four

Underlying Psychological Disorders and Comorbid Conditions

While a functional model of school refusal allows us to identify the purpose that the school refusal serves, we cannot simply stop there. The first analytical or diagnostic decision is to identify the purpose or function of the school refusal, but that is not sufficient to effectively intervene. This point may be best illustrated by a case example.

Bob and Bill are both refusing school as an attempt to avoid the social and evaluative components of school. In both situations it is clear and they can articulate that they "just don't fit in." Bob, in addition to his school refusal has an IQ of 155, is an Olympic class gymnast, has won awards for creative writing, and has very supportive and understanding parents. Bill also refuses school for the same purpose of avoiding the social aspects of attendance, but has an IQ of 80, has a significant reading disability, is periodically enuretic, has consistently received failing grades, and his father is in jail and his mother has a significant substance abuse problem.

In both situations, the school refusal has at its purpose the avoidance or escape from the social or evaluative component of school attendance. A "one size fits all" approach to Bob's and Bill's school refusal, even one based on a thorough understanding of the purpose and function of the refusal behavior, is unlikely to be successful without a second analytical or diagnostic analysis. This second process must identify any underlying psychological disorders and comorbid conditions creating, exacerbating, or impacting the school refusal behaviors. This second level analysis has as its purpose identifying any psychopathology or serious emotional issues which might be contributing to or is causative of the school refusal behavior. In many instances it may be necessary to first address the underlying conditions before any substantive progress can be made on dealing with the school refusal.

Separation Anxiety Disorder

One frequently observed underlying condition associated with school refusal is Separation Anxiety Disorder. The *DSM-IV-TR (2000)* describes Separation Anxiety Disorder as a disorder occurring prior to age 18 where the individual becomes excessively anxious when separated from parents or home. Symptoms of anxiety must have occurred for a period of at least 4 weeks. Often the child displays excessive worries, fears, distress, nightmares, and obsessive thinking about being separated from home or primary caregivers. The reaction is excessive and any anticipated separation may produce somatic complaints. Onset of Separation Anxiety occurs normally during preschool years and occurs in approximately 4% of all children. The disorder is more common among first-degree relatives and in children of parents with Panic Disorder. A level of separation anxiety is normal for children between 18 months and 3 years, but by 4, most children do not continue to show symptoms. Four percent of children continue beyond age 4 and only one percent continue to be symptomatic by ages 14-16 (*DSM-IV-TR*, 2000).

34

Many of these youth are excessively miserable when not with loved ones, preoccupied with fears about health and safety of parents, and avoid going places on their own. Children dealing with excessive separation anxiety may be reluctant or refuse to participate in sleepovers, demand that someone stay with them at bedtime or sleep with them, and/or may experience recurring nightmares about being separated from parents. This can be a significant part of school refusal behaviors as a logical extension of their already dysfunctional anxiety level. When forced to separate from parents in order to attend school, these youth may become preoccupied with their parents' whereabouts, prompting requests for unnecessary phone contact. They can also be so threatened and preoccupied about being separated from their parents that they are unable to perform in the classroom at an acceptable level. The child who is obsessing about the idea that his mother might have an accident on the way home is unlikely to be able to function in the classroom, and as the separation anxiety builds, it may prompt pleas to make a phone call, an upset stomach, headache, other maladies, or disruptive behavior in the classroom.

Children who suffer from Separation Anxiety Disorder may also engage in disruptive behaviors in the classroom setting to force parental contact. They frequently create situations in the morning at home which may delay going to school or prevent attendance entirely. Part of the symptom repertoire, which those youth struggling with separation anxiety may use to avoid school attendance, is through the display of a number of vague somatic symptoms. These children may have frequent complaints of dizziness, nausea, cramps, vomiting, palpitations, etc., even to the point that symptoms are inconsistent or physically impossible, i.e. "I feel sick at my stomach, but I'm starving to death.

Generalized Anxiety Disorder (Overanxious Disorder of Childhood)

Many youth who struggle with school refusal may also struggle with Generalized Anxiety Disorder (GAD) as identified in the *DSM-IV-TR (2000)*. Although they do not experience episodes of acute panic, these individuals feel tense or anxious most of the time and find it difficult to control their worries. Their uncontrollable worry may relate to school attendance or be less specific and more generally pervasive. Criteria for Generalized Anxiety Disorder call for the condition to have existed in excess of six months and that the individual experiences less specific bodily symptoms than other anxiety disorders. Symptoms may involve restlessness, fatigue, and difficulty concentrating, irritability, muscle tension, and sleep disturbances. It includes what had formerly been called the Overanxious Disorder of Childhood. For many children and adolescents, their anxieties typically involve non-specific issues around competence, performance, catastrophic events, perfectionism, and lack of approval.

Youth with Generalized Anxiety Disorder may worry excessively about their ability to perform satisfactorily at school. This excessive worry and discomfort may result in a number of escape or avoidance behaviors, including school refusal behaviors. Some children may be excessively focused on perfection to the point that they cannot adequately conform to the expectations of the classroom. Their concern about perfectionism may result in requiring excessive time or effort to complete basic assignments. School becomes an activity where they are frequently reminded of their inability to achieve perfection and is viewed as a source of frustration and failure which should be avoided at all costs. If the Generalized Anxiety is untreated, it is unlikely that the child will ever develop sufficient comfort with the school experience to attend regularly.

Specific Phobia (formerly Simple Phobia)

Individuals with Specific Phobias fear specific objects or situations (e.g. animals, storms, closed spaces) and react excessively and disproportionately to the phobic object or situation. *DSM-IV-TR (2000)* criteria specify that the person often recognizes the fear as unreasonable, but still avoids the specific stimuli, or endures it with intense distress. For children it must be of at least six months duration. Some youth may not recognize their fear as excessive and it may be expressed non-verbally through crying, tantrums, freezing, or clinging. Specific fears in children are fairly normal, but in most situations, the fears fade with development or gradual exposure to the feared situation or object. A phobic reaction to the stimuli of "school" as a generic concept is frequently observed, but a differential must be made between Specific Phobia (germs, an animal in the classroom) Social Phobia (no one there likes me and they make fun of me), and Separation Anxiety (separation from a "safe person," place, or object). Realistic childhood fears are developmentally appropriate and a distinction must be made based on the level with which the Specific Phobia interferes with functioning and the length of time which the phobia has persisted.

Social Phobia (Social Anxiety Disorder)

Many school refusers have significant issues with Social Phobia or a Social Anxiety Disorder (Kearney, 2005). These individuals fear embarrassment or humiliation in social or performance situations. The individual recognizes that the fear is excessive and that it interferes with normal functioning. In children, there must be evidence of the capacity for age appropriate social relationships and the anxiety must occur in peer settings, not just with adults. Children do not always recognize that their fear is excessive and the anxiety may be expressed non-verbally through crying, tantrums, and freezing or shrinking from unfamiliar people. Some consideration must be given to the level of social exposure which the child has had in the past and whether or not the child has demonstrated the ability to socially interact appropriately in other situations with individuals whom they have a greater familiarity and exposure (*DSM-IV-TR, 2000*).

Panic Attacks

A Panic Attack is a brief episode where the individual feels intense dread, accompanied by a variety of extreme physical symptoms. It begins suddenly and peaks rapidly. The onset of the attacks and the presence of "triggers" are important. Three types of panic reactions are observed: unexpected (e.g. Panic Disorder), situational bound (e.g. Phobias), or situational predisposed (e.g. PTSD). *Panic disorders are rarely seen in children until late adolescence*, and the onset of panic disorder typically occurs in 20's to 30's (*DSM-IV-TR, 2000*). In working with younger children, they may experience "freak outs" and "meltdowns," but it would be rare for young children to experience the physiological extremes which typically occur in adults with Panic Disorder. In older adolescents, particularly those with a family history of Panic Disorder or panic attacks, some prodromal signs of a developing Panic Disorder may be observed.

Obsessive Compulsive Disorder

Obsessive Compulsive Disorder can create particular difficulties for some children who ultimately refuse school as a way of managing their obsessive compulsive rituals and thinking. Individuals with Obsessive Compulsive Disorder are bothered by repeated thoughts and behaviors which seem senseless, even to them, but somehow make them feel less anxious and more comfortable (*DSM-IV-TR*, 2000). This recognition of the excessiveness or unreasonableness does not always occur with children. If the school setting blocks or makes it extremely difficult for the child to engage in their anxiety reducing rituals, school may be avoided or refused. While the obsessions (thoughts or images) cause distress, the compulsions (actions) prevent, reduce, or relieve anxiety. Obsessive Compulsive Disorder may take the form of *either* obsessions or compulsions, but normally, both are present. Washing, checking, counting, and ordering rituals are particularly common with children.

The relationship between school refusal and Obsessive Compulsive Disorder is readily seen in the following example. *Megan was diagnosed at a relatively young age with Obsessive Compulsive Disorder. As an adolescent she has found ways of concealing many of her compulsions in ways which are more socially acceptable. However, one set of compulsive behaviors, which she has not been able to give up or conceal, is her need to have her appearance absolutely perfect before she can leave for school. This often results in dressing and redressing multiple times to the point that she misses the bus, is late for school, or completely shuts down and refuses to go to school, "because she can't get her hair to look right."* Until the Obsessive Compulsive Disorder is addressed either through behavior modification, medication, and/or both, it is unlikely that the school refusal behaviors can be addressed successfully.

Post Traumatic Stress Disorder

Many children who are school refusers have suffered significant trauma at school or in the school context. The child who has been assaulted at school, the child who was humiliated by classmates or teachers, the child who was sexually abused at school, the child who was verbally or emotionally abused by a teacher may be experiencing Post Traumatic Stress Disorder or PTSD. Post Traumatic Stress Disorder is observed in individuals who have experienced, witnessed, or been confronted with an event involving threat of death, serious injury, or loss of physical integrity (sexual abuse). The person's response to the event involved fear, helplessness, or horror and these individuals continue to experience the fear and anxiety in a repetitive fashion when triggered by similar stimuli or stimuli reminiscent of the original trauma (*DSM-IV-TR*, 2000).

In children, Post Traumatic Stress Disorder is often expressed by disorganized or agitated behavior. The youth re-experiences the trauma, avoids stimuli (or is unresponsive to stimuli) associated with the trauma, and experiences a level of increased arousal. In children, repetitive play, with themes or aspects of the trauma may be expressed. There may be frightening dreams without recognizable content, or trauma specific reenactment may occur (*DSM-IV-TR*, 2000). While the school setting may be the source of the original trauma, we continue to expect and require the child to attend school and run the risk of being further traumatized. As the trauma response becomes intensified, the child may refuse school as a coping mechanism.

Children may have been exposed to violence, assaults, threats, intimidation, and physical or sexual abuse in the school setting or in the school buildings or on school grounds. If not directly exposed, the media may have exposed them by coverage of school violence to the point that the child actually perceives a legitimate threat to their life and safety by being in the school building. Until the PTSD symptoms have been resolved, requiring the child to attend school may lead to additional traumatization and increased avoidance behaviors.

Major Depressive Episode

Depression, and the accompanying loss of energy and anhedonia, may make attending school very difficult for many children. Issues of sleep irregularities, loss of appetite or increased appetite, and difficulties with concentration are an integral part of a Major Depressive Episode and may ultimately result in a child's inability to attend school. In children, a major depressive episode is more likely to occur in conjunction with other disorders (Oppositional Defiant, Conduct Disorder, ADHD, and Anxiety Disorders) than in isolation, making attending school on a regular basis extremely difficult. Major Depression is less common in children than in adults, particularly prepubertal children, but has generally been under diagnosed in children (*DSM-IV-TR*, 2000). In children, the affective state may be an irritable, "agitated depression" rather than the depressed mood or loss of interest in activities typically observed in depressed adults.

Some children may lack sufficient capacity for self-reflection and self-observation to be able to identify their affective state as depression. A not yet fully developed concept of time or the future may also make identification of what they are experiencing difficult. Many children may have a family history replete with individuals who have experienced significant Major Depressive Episodes and it is very likely that they may be experiencing prodromal physical and neurological symptoms of depression without being capable of accurately labeling them. These prodromal symptoms may make school attendance very difficult and may ultimately result in school refusal behaviors.

Oppositional Defiant Disorder

Oppositional Defiant Disorder may be the underlying cause in many instances of school refusal. The refusal to be compliant with the wishes and direction of adults is the hallmark of Oppositional Defiant Disorder (ODD). What more direct and age appropriate manner of expressing opposition and lack of compliance to adult wishes than to engage in school refusal behaviors. Refusing to attend school is a primary opportunity for the ODD child to be oppositional and resistive to adult wishes and directives. ODD children often display multiple examples of negativistic, defiant, disobedient, and hostile behaviors which have been occurring for a period of more than six months. This can often be seen in very young children, but should be diagnosed with the recognition of normal developmental oppositionalism (*DSM-IV-TR, 2000*). Onset is typically gradual, occurring over the course of months or years. It is frequently observed in the children of families with serious marital discord, substance abuse, or a primary caretaker who struggles with depression.

Conduct Disorder

Children who refuse school initially as a product of their Oppositional Defiant Disorder may continue to develop more significant behavioral issues, which may ultimately reach the level of a Conduct Disorder (*DSM-IV-TR*, 2000). In many situations, there is a fairly predictable progression from Oppositional Defiant Disorder to Conduct Disorder to Antisocial Personality Disorder. Conduct Disordered children typically violate the rights of others, particularly in terms of aggression, destruction of property, lying, stealing, and serious rules violations. In a number of ways, the Conduct Disorder bears a strong resemblance to and may be viewed as a possible precursor to an Antisocial Personality Disorder (a kid version of ASPD).

The repetitive and persistent nature of the behavior distinguishes it from an adjustment disorder. Understandably, this disorder involves aggression, destructiveness, deceit, or theft, and violation of rules and expectations. One of the specific diagnostic criteria for a Conduct Disorder is a failure to attend school "often truant from school, beginning before age 13 years" (*DSM-TR-IV*, 2000). Almost all cases which meet the criteria for Conduct Disorder would also meet criteria for Oppositional Defiant Disorder, however, the converse is not necessarily true. In addition, while almost all individuals who are ultimately diagnosed with an Antisocial Personality Disorder were very likely identified as progressing from Oppositional Defiant Disorder to Conduct Disorder to Antisocial Personality Disorder, the reverse is not necessarily true.

Encopresis and Enuresis

For a child who struggles with enuresis and encopresis, the thought of attending school and having an "accident" in a public setting can create sufficient anxiety to make attending school very difficult. A child may refuse to attend school as a safe way of avoiding embarrassment, shame, and ridicule. The anticipatory anxiety, which comes with even the thought of attending school and not being able to successfully regulate bowel and bladder, may actually increase the possibility of the loss of bowel or bladder control. School refusers may be opting out of school rather than run the risk of an embarrassing event.

Attention Deficit/ Hyperactivity Disorder

For a child with Attention Deficit/Hyperactivity Disorder (ADHD), attending school might be considered "cruel and unusual punishment." For the entire school day, the child will be asked to comply in ways which they find difficult, if not impossible. They will be subject to ongoing correction, criticism, critique, and negative messages about them, their behavior, and their performance. It would stand to reason that some of these children may "opt out" and either refuse to attend school

44

completely or be unable or unwilling to participate in the educational processes for an entire day and engage in some form of escape behaviors, such as school refusal.

Attention Deficit/Hyperactivity Disorder has had a variety of names and descriptions since it was first described in 1902 and is one of the most commonly diagnosed disorders of childhood (*DSM-IV-TR*, 2000). It is a composite disorder including two major symptoms: inattention and impulsivity/hyperactivity. It is especially difficult to establish this diagnosis in children younger than four, although symptoms can be observed. Younger children typically experience few demands for sustained attention until the school setting. Criteria call for symptoms to have occurred prior to age seven and for symptoms to occur in two or more settings and not exclusively at school. Mothers of ADHD children frequently report higher intrauterine activity, excessive crying, sleep issues, and increased irritability (*DSM-IV-TR*, 2000).

Developmental milestones occur early and these children "hit the ground running." They appear to be "motor-driven" and often engage in daredevil and risky activities. They may perform poorly in school, though IQ is typically in the normal range. There is a significant correlation between first degree family members and individuals diagnosed with ADHD. A family history of mood disorders, learning disabilities, substance abuse, and antisocial behavior is often observed. *DSM-IV-TR (2000)* identifies four specific types of ADHD:

- Attention Deficit/Hyperactivity Disorder, Combined Type where the criteria for both inattention and hyperactivity/impulsivity are met;
- Attention Deficit/Hyperactivity Disorder, Predominantly Inattentive Type where the

criteria for inattention but not hyperactivity/impulsivity are met;

- Attention Deficit/Hyperactivity Disorder, Predominantly Hyperactive/Impulsive Type where the criteria for hyperactivity/impulsivity but not inattention are met;
- and, Attention Deficit/Hyperactivity Disorder Not Otherwise Specified where there are prominent atypical symptoms of inattention or hyperactivity/impulsivity.

Learning Disorders

A significant comorbid condition, which directly impacts school refusal behavior, is the presence of a Learning Disorder. Learning disorders are characterized by inadequate development of academic skills which are not due to demonstrable physical or neurological disorders. Criteria for a Learning Disorder as outlined in the *DSM-IV-TR (2000)*, requires that academic achievement be *substantially* below what would be expected given the person's age, IQ, and educational level. Estimates are that between 2 to 10 percent of the population meet the criteria and approximately 5 percent of students in public schools are identified as having a learning disorder. Attending school is likely to be extremely frustrating for these youth as they may not be able to meet or measure up to the expectations for normal achievement and academic progress. Many of these youth are labeled or targeted for ridicule by their peers who are well aware that the child is not progressing academically. Many of these learning disabled children may avoid the negative experiences of school, which are almost inevitable for a learning disabled child, by refusing to attend or other negative and self-defeating coping strategies.

Chapter Five

Diagnostic and Assessment Issues of School Refusers

In addition to those diagnosable comorbid conditions discussed earlier, many school refusers have a variety of underlying conditions which may cause, exacerbate, or reinforce refusal to attend school. In order to successfully intervene, these individual characteristics, environmental, or extenuating factors must be identified and successfully addressed in order for an intervention to be successful and to prevent relapses from occurring (Kearney & Albano, 2007). Absent a clear identification of all underlying conditions, many interventions with a school refusing youth are doomed to have limited success or will only succeed for a limited time until the child adopts other, alternative means of avoiding attendance at school.

Several aspects of an accurate assessment become even more critical for school refusers. Due to the significant somatization, which many of these children display, it is essential to obtain a complete medical history and a thorough physical examination. While many of the school refuser's somatic symptoms are indications of malingering or psychosomatic in nature, some children may be experiencing significant physical symptoms or organically based difficulties. A child who has had no real issues with attending school, but who suddenly sleeps constantly, lacks energy, has a variety of physical complaints, aches, and pains may be malingering or developing psychosomatic illnesses to justify his or her failure to attend. The same set of physical symptoms being observed may also be a behavioral description of a child suffering from mononucleosis. Thyroid conditions, diabetes, lead/mercury exposure, anemia, and seizures may all be physical disorders which have resulted in an inability to attend school physically, rather than school refusal behavior.

It is also critical to conduct separate interviews with parents and the child (Kearney and Albano, 2007). Many of these children come from extremely enmeshed families and often there exists a version of "unispeak" where the parent speaks for the child or the child speaks for the parents. Conducting a separate interview with the child and parents allows for greater insight into the behavior that is actually taking place. Kearney and Albano (2007) suggested that "as a general rule in cases of school refusal behavior, interview the child before the parents." They also provided a structured set of questions for the child and parent to answer separately, which may provide some insight as to the nature and purpose of the school refusal behavior.

Part of the assessment process will attempt to identify the purpose of the school refusal (functional model), but in addition, there must be a clear understanding and evaluation of other factors maintaining school refusal behaviors. In order for the behavior to continue to persist, there must be a reinforcing contingency at work. Any intervention strategy must address the reinforcers of inappropriate behavior. Determining the possibility of secondary gains produced by the school refusal behavior, and the manner in which those occur, will be a key toward developing an effective intervention plan and preventing relapses.

For many school refusing children, a strong underlying component of their school refusal is anxiety and depression (Last & Strauss, 1990). School refusal may be an extended symptom of underlying anxiety or depression and must always

48

be considered when assessing a school refusing child. Many of these children have such strong underlying anxiety issues that the nature of the chaos, confusion, and excitement of a normal school day may create sensory overloading which amounts to an intolerable level of stress. It would not be unusual for many school refusers to arrive at school each day, and as the day progresses, the anxiety builds and builds until it reaches a point of critical mass. At the point when their anxiety becomes unbearable, the child then resorts to some form of escape or avoidance behaviors. These behaviors may result in their going home or spending the day in the health room or nurse's office.

In addition, for many school refusers, a pattern of family dysfunction may be creating or exacerbating the school refusal behavior. Some parents may be active participants in encouraging school refusal behaviors to meet their own individual needs or the needs of the family. Others, while not consciously encouraging school refusal, may be collaborators in avoidance of attending school (Kearney & Silverman, 1995). It would, however, be faulty to assume that all school refusers come from dysfunctional families. Many school refusers have families that are perfectly healthy and functional, but there may be specific stimuli about the school experience which produces inappropriate coping strategies.

In assessing school refusers it is important to note any pattern of school absence. The child who consistently misses school on Thursdays may be communicating that some event or person is only experienced on that particular day. It could be gym class, art class, or contact with a bully which only occurs on Thursday. A careful review, may provide information about the exact intervention required. In addition it would also be important to carefully review the time period of the first onset of the problem. Answers to the proverbial "Why here? Why now?"

49

questions may provide significant information required for a successful intervention.

Kearney (2008b) identified a number of contextual issues that have to be considered when attempting to intervene with a child who is a school refuser, including: homelessness and poverty, teenage pregnancy, school violence, school bullying, and *school climate*. He defines school climate as "the student's feelings of connectedness to the school and the degree of support of their academic and other needs." School climate is the match or "goodness of fit" between the student's unique academic needs and interests and the curriculum and educational programs. A poor match may create a climate where school refusal exists and will continue to exist without appropriate modifications or a better match. Kearney (2008b) states that "this is especially important for youths with learning problems who are at special risk for school refusal behaviors."

Obtaining collateral information from other people who know or have interactions with the child may also provide a direction as to the purpose of the school refusal and the factors which reinforce or support the behavior. Standardized measures which assess functioning levels and underlying conditions may also be a key supplement to existing information. Standardized measures, which evaluate the level of anxiety or level of depression a child is experiencing, will put any intervention plan on a much firmer footing and guarantee a higher success rate when intervening with school refusers. Some of the more commonly used standardized measures might include:

Social Anxiety Scale for Children/Adolescents - assesses fear of negative evaluation and social avoidance and distress.

Child Behavior Checklist (Achenbach) - Children who refuse school to escape aversive social or evaluative situations show significantly higher scores on Withdrawal and Somatic Complaints Scales, as well as the overall Internalizing Scale.

Behavioral Assessment System for Children (BASC) - provides a measure of Internalizing vs. Externalizing problems as they relate to school refusal.

State-Trait Anxiety Inventory for Children - a 40 item inventory which distinguishes situational based anxiety from characterological anxiety.

Manifest Anxiety Scale - a 37 item, yes/no inventory which targets physiological anxiety, worry, and concentration difficulties. It is useful for children who refuse school to avoid negative situations (escape behaviors).

Reynolds Child/Adolescent Depression Scale - measures depressive symptoms and is particularly useful for children who refuse school to avoid general negative affectivity or to escape evaluative situations.

Anxiety Disorders Interview Schedule for the DSM-IV-TR - offers a parent and child version and a special section on school refusal related problems.

School Refusal Assessment Scale - features Parent and Child Questionnaires to determine the function of the school refusal behavior (Graywind Publications).

Strategic Intervention Planning

Strategic Intervention with school refusers must be based on decisions and information arrived at during the assessment and diagnostic process. Intervention plans should describe outcomes you wish to achieve and the interventions you plan to use to reduce, relieve, ameliorate, or change the symptoms (distress) or impairment (loss of functioning).

By asking yourself "What" questions about the individual, the goals of the intervention can be determined. (e.g. What is the most distressing aspect of the school refusal? What physical factors may contribute to the situation or exacerbate the refusal? What stressor is the individual experiencing? What underlying conditions must be addressed? etc.)

The objectives of the intervention plan specify the "How" goals are to be addressed and the interventions that will be attempted (e.g. How can attendance be increased? How will the learning disability be addressed? How will the client learn to express anger effectively? How will marital tension be reduced? How will family and teachers monitor change? etc.)

Establishing a strategic intervention plan for a child with school refusal behaviors is critical due to the fact that school refusal behavior is not a single factor disorder or syndrome but takes various shapes, forms, purposes, and outcomes. School refusers, as a group are one of the most non-homogeneous groups of individuals who share a common label. Any effective intervention must be based on a thorough assessment of the purpose of the behavior, identifying any underlying or comorbid conditions, and targeting any factors which maintain, exacerbate, or reinforce the school refusal behavior. An effective, individualized intervention plan is a four step process: 1) identifying the purpose that the school refusal serves, 2) identifying underlying or comorbid conditions, 3) establishing tentative goals to be accomplished to successfully intervene, and 4) creating objectives which will lead to the accomplishment of the intervention goals.

An example of a Strategic Intervention Plan for a child engaging in school refusal behavior follows:

Type of School Refusal: *School Refusal for Attention Seeking (AS)*

Underlying or Comorbid Conditions: 309.*21*
Separation Anxiety, Early Onset, Possible Gastro-intestinal Concerns, and Parental Conflict

Goal I: Decrease Excessive Anxiety Concerning Separation

Objective A: Explore precipitating events such as losses, stressors, and changes through individual therapy.

Objective B: Deal with issues related to rational fears through problem solving and teaching coping skills.

Objective C: Confront irrational fears and beliefs through cognitive therapy.

Objective D: Minimize the psychological impact of anxiety by teaching relaxation training and self-talk strategies.

Goal II: Increase School Attendance and Achievement

Objective A: Increase school and parent consistency through conducting joint meeting with parents, school personnel, and child.

Objective B: Develop a "morning routine" which will be followed by the parents without regard to the child's behavior.

Objective C: Develop a consistent and predictable strategy for assisting the child from the car to the classroom.

Objective D: Develop a system of "anxiety strategies" which can be deployed in the classroom to prevent withdrawal through access to support personnel or "worry time."

Goal III: Explore Physical Symptoms

Objective A: Conduct a complete physical to rule out any organic basis for vomiting or headaches.

Goal IV: Reduce Parental Conflict

Objective A: Parents will participate in marital therapy to learn effective strategies for conflict resolution.
Objective B: Educate parents regarding age appropriate emotional separation through parenting classes.

Goal V: Increase Overall Level of Functioning

Objective A: Increase, through systematic desensitization, the amount of time the child can tolerate being away from the parent.
Objective B: Develop a list of coping strategies that the child can employ to avoid feeling anxious when separated through a family brainstorming process.

Goal VI: Involve Other Family Members as Supports

Objective A: Increase anxiety free time away from parents by utilizing his favorite Uncle to serve as a security object.
Objective B: Increase capacity to be away from parents through sleepovers at cousin's hous

Chapter Six

General Intervention Approaches

The treatment or intervention of choice with a school refuser is **as early a return to school as possible** (Kearney & Silverman, 1999). The number one factor increasing the likelihood of success with children who can't or won't go to school is an early return to the physical environment of school. Quickly returning to attending some portion of the school day is the most effective intervention in almost all situations. The longer the child successfully remains outside the school and outside a normal school day routine, the more difficult it will be to return to school. Identifying particular classes which the child can attend, identifying a limited time period where the child is required to be in the building, or identifying certain days which the child must attend are all legitimate strategies to employ and legitimate starting points for development of more comprehensive intervention goals and objectives.

This may require some flexibility on the part of school officials to give "tacit" approval of a child not being present for the entire day. *Even with a partial return to school, the ultimate goal is attending for a full day on a regular and consistent basis.* A plan should be in place to gradually increase attendance to a more normal pattern and not just continue the alterations indefinitely. Identifying a gradually increasing expectation for normal attendance pattern does not allow the child to become totally comfortable with a modified schedule. The partial or full return to school may also be dependent on some environmental shifts. This will require cooperation of school administration, such as a schedule change, a teacher change, allowing the child to arrive at the school through another entrance, allowing the child to arrive early, or allowing them to arrive late. In these situations it is important to insure that the school administration is in agreement with the intervention plan and the steps to achieving full attendance. Mutual agreement on the part of both parents as well as mutual agreement with school officials on a strategy of partial return is critical to prevent the child from "splitting" parents or "splitting" parents and school personnel.

The following discussion of intervention strategies looks first at some general approaches or interventions frequently employed with this population and then looks at specific interventions that work most effectively with the four different purposes which school refusal might be serving.

General Approaches

Systematic Desensitization

The process of systematic desensitization is a long-standing behavioral strategy for dealing with an anxiety based fear response which is out of proportion to the actual stimuli. For many school refusers, their anxiety about attending school is often far in excess of what even they identify as reasonable. Systematic desensitization is the process of developing a fear producing stimulus hierarchy of the feared aspects of attending school and then systematically pairing the items on the hierarchy with deep muscle progressive relaxation which is incompatible with an anxiety based response. Gradually working the child through her hierarchy of fears related to school and giving her the ability to regulate her response to the feared situation may allow the child to return to school (King at al., 1998).

Exposure Therapy

Exposure Therapy has at its core the idea that habituation will occur with continued or prolonged exposure to an anxiety provoking stimuli. With a school refuser, the goal is to extinguish or diminish the fear response to attending school through continual exposure. The exposure to the feared object (hallways, teacher, gym class, bathrooms, etc.) can be *in vivo* with the idea of a gradual reentry to school and easing the child back into a classroom situation with longer periods of exposure. Another exposure therapy approach is the idea of implosion or flooding. This is a rapid reentry or exposure, with the assumption that the person subjected to prolonged exposure to the feared object or situation will eventually habituate.

Modeling Therapy

Modeling and Role Playing for school refusers has been particularly effective for those youth who struggle with the social aspects of the school experience. Based on social learning theory, the premise is that by demonstrating or showing the child non-fearful behavior options in anxiety provoking situations, they may be able to copy the behaviors and develop a repertoire of responses which will allow them to function in an anxiety provoking situation. The modeling opportunity can be presented in a number of formats including, video modeling, live modeling, and participant modeling where the child observes another child modeling non-anxious behaviors and then performs the behaviors with the aid of the therapist. This "seeing and then doing" approach has been most effective (Terry, 1998). In a less formal or structured way, simply engaging in role playing activities and receiving immediate feedback can also have a very positive effect.

Cognitive Therapy

Cognitive therapy assumes that the child perceives some aspect of school attendance as threatening (to the child, caregiver, or family) and feels incapable of managing the situation. By remaining at home, the problem is avoided, anxiety is reduced, and school refusal is reinforced. Cognitive Behavior Therapy (CBT) has been shown to be effective in treating school refusal (King et al., 1998 and Last, Hansen, & Franco, 1998). Wimmer (2003) reports that 83% of children with school refusal behaviors treated with cognitive therapy were attending school at a one year follow-up.

Silverman et al (2008) have concluded that sufficient information is available to include Cognitive Behavioral Therapy as fitting criteria as a *Possibly Efficacious Treatment* for school refusal. A large part of doing cognitive therapy with this population is likely to involve Cognitive Restructuring. Assisting the child to identify self-statements which result in anxiety and then providing them with a counter, contrasting the anxiety provoking statements with alternative positive statements, is a way of effectively changing many of the cognitive distortions at the root of their anxiety. The new cognitions may take the form of a mantra which can be repeated subauditorially to decrease anxiety. Having the child keep a daily *Behavioral and Thought Diary* can provide some insight into the cognitive distortions which produce the anxious feelings.

Social Skills Training

Providing the child who struggles with the social aspects of school with concrete skills and techniques to increase their ability to function in a social context may be a key

59

to eliminating school refusal. Social skills can be taught in a variety of concrete ways and utilizing a variety of formats. Social skills groups of age level peers where a child can receive feedback about her social behaviors are very effective. Having a trusted adult who serves as a "social coach" is also effective by encouraging a child to engage in a more socially accepted way and to have an experience of a positive social encounter at school. Verbal skills and strategies which increase social effectiveness can be taught and encouraged. In addition, teaching school refusing children to be aware of and accurately read non-verbal cues and signs will increase social effectiveness (Kearney, 2008a).

Parent Training

For the group of school refusers whose purpose is attention seeking behavior (ASB), the bulk of the intervention may be assisting the parents and school personnel in changing their patterns of interaction with the child (Kearney, 2007a). School refusal behavior is often a polarizing experience for parents who may have very different ideas and approaches for handling the problem. Parental involvement is a key indicator for success, because as long as the parents do not present a united front and a consistent approach to the issue, the child will continue to divide and receive enormous attention, sympathy, and involvement of one of his parents. Parent training often provides parents with a broader range of parenting options and behavioral management strategies. Parent training may also have the benefit of a reduction in a parent's own anxiety which will make them considerably more effective in intervening with their child.

Educational/Supportive Therapy

Providing children and their parents with information about the nature of anxiety can be an effective intervention for some school refusers. For a child, just understanding what is happening to them and normalizing anxiety as a part of life can provide them the opportunity to make a different response to attending school. Helping a child to talk about fears and distinguish between fear, anxiety, and phobias can alleviate some of the panicky feelings they experience in school. For some older children journaling about fears, thoughts, and coping strategies is an effective tool.

Pharmacological Treatments

In many situations, the pediatrician and a medication approach to the problem of school refusal is the first line of defense. Occasionally medication is the only intervention or medications are used in conjunction with behavioral and psychotherapy interventions. Some authors have strong opinions that medication has no place in the treatment of school refusal (Kearney, 2001 and Kearney & Albano, 2007). Some of the more typical medications utilized include:

- **Tricyclics** – Imipramine may be useful in some cases (Bernstein et al., 2000). Studies have indicated that a tricyclic antidepressant may be more useful for children with better attendance records and fewer symptoms of social avoidance and separation anxiety (Kearney, 2006b).
- **SSRIs** – Prozac (only SSRI approved for use with children under 12), Paxil, Zoloft, Luvox, and other SSRI's are not recommended for

children with a family history of Bi-Polar Disorder (Seidel & Walkup, 2006)

- **Beta Blockers** – Inderal (Propranolol) is effective at managing the physical symptoms of anxiety. Abrupt cessation of use may trigger a hypertensive crisis.
- **Benzodiazepines** – Ativan, Valium, Xanax may present possible physical and/or psychological addiction. Benzodiazepines are not first line treatment because of concerns about dependence, withdrawal, and drug tolerance (Last & Strauss, 1990). Because of the side effects and risk of dependence, benzodiazepines should be used for only a few weeks, if at all (Riddle et al., 1999).

Kearney and Albano (2007) have expressed several specific concerns about using medications as the primary intervention for those youth struggling with school refusal. Their belief is that medication may be appropriate in those cases where the level of stress and duress is extremely high, but may actually be detrimental for those school refusers whose distress is in a mid range or low range. While children with extremely high levels of distress may respond well, those with moderate distress may be unresponsive or may be plagued by considerable side effects (Kearney, 2006b). While medication may be effective at moderating the physical feelings of distress, they have limited or no impact on the "thinking" or "acting" aspects of their distress. A child on medication may feel physically better, but may still obsess about thoughts of not wanting to attend school or the negative aspects of attending school. Medication may have little impact on well established escape behaviors which are firmly established through a reinforcement schedule that is self-defeating, even though the child feels less physical distress while they are refusing to attend school (Kearney & Silverman, 1998).

Family Therapy

Family therapy with school refusers may be a very effective intervention. Typical family therapy allows for an exploration of the purpose that the school refusal might serve in maintaining the equilibrium within the family system. Family therapy, rather than focusing on the pathology or emotional issues of the school refuser, attempts to identify the ways which the family might be inadvertently or unknowingly rewarding, reinforcing, or encouraging school refusal. There are many different forms of family therapy, but most have some dimension of examining the roles each family member plays, responsibilities carried by a family member, the power dynamic within the family, and family communication patterns. In addition typical family therapy explores the family routines, the unwritten family rules, and who in the family has the power to reward or regulate behavior. Many times a change in family dynamics or family functioning will extinguish school refusal behavior in a family member.

Alternative Instruction

In some situations, the use of alternatives to traditional school based instruction may need to be employed. These situations should be viewed as temporary and transitional and not as a resolution to the problem, as the primary treatment goal is an early return to school. Homebound instruction, online school, or other alternative instruction processes will not resolve the school refusal behavioral issues. In some cases, the extra attention may make staying at home more attractive and actually reinforce the school refusal behavior. Home schooling may mask the anxiety, but does not deal with the underlying anxiety, and may actually result in further socially isolating the child.

The following is a chart complied by Kearney and Albano (2000) identifying a number of intervention strategies most suited for each of the four types of school refusers.

Treatment of School Refusal	
Function	*Treatment Components*
To avoid stimuli that provoke general negative affect (SPNA) (crying, nausea, distress, sadness, and various phobias, i.e. bathrooms, cafeteria, teachers, bullies, etc.)	Somatic control exercises such as breathing retraining and muscle relaxation Gradual re-exposure to school Reduce physical symptoms and anticipatory anxiety Self-reinforcement, self-talk, self-esteem
To escape aversive social and evaluative situations (EASE) (social phobia, test anxiety, shyness, lack of social skills)	Role play Cognitive restructuring of negative self-talk Gradual exposure to real life situations Social skills training and reduction of social anxiety Coping strategies templates
To get attention (ASB) (tantrums, crying, clinging, separation anxiety)	Parent training in contingency management Clear parental messages Evening and morning routines Use of consequences for compliance/noncompliance Forced Attendance
For positive tangible reinforcement (TROS) (lack of structure or rules, free access to reinforcement, avoidance of limits)	Family contingency contracting to increase rewards for attending school and decrease rewards for missing school Curtail social and other activities for nonattendance Alternative problem solving

Evidence for Utilizing Interventions Based on a Functional Model of School Refusal

The Functional Model of school refusal is based on a prescriptive identification of the purpose of the school refusal and would appear to meet criteria to be considered an evidence based treatment approach. The approach has been tested in uncontrolled and controlled studies of prescriptive and nonprescriptive treatment (Chorpita et al.,1996; Kearney, 2002b and 2007b; Kearney, Pursell, & Alvarez, 2001; Kearney & Silverman, 1990, 1999). Kearney and Silverman (1999) found that key measures in the functional model could accurately predict which prescriptive or tailored treatments would be effective for a particular case.

Recent data supports the use of a Functional Model of school refusal behavior. Among a sample of 222 youths with school refusal behaviors, Kearney (2007b) demonstrated that utilizing a structural model to find the function of school refusal was a better predictor of school absenteeism than traditional measures of fear, anxiety, and depression. Wimmer (2003) reported that 83% of children with school refusal behaviors treated with cognitive therapy were attending school at one year follow-up.

Silverman et al. (2008) have concluded that there is sufficient data to conclude that a cognitive behavior therapy approach such as the Functional Model of School Refusal meets the criteria to be considered *Possibly Efficacious*.

However, Kearney and Albano (2007) also recognized the need for ongoing research and further validation of this approach: "*Although the procedures have been shown to be highly useful for youth with psychopathology and school refusal behavior, the functional model remains in development. As such we encourage clinicians to utilize our guidelines with appropriate caution. In addition clinicians should consider recommending adjunctive treatments such as medication, family therapy, or educational interventions for learning disorders or classroom misbehavior as appropriate and necessary."*

The following information attempts to look at the phenomenon of school refusal and the specific interventions which work most effectively with the four different purposes that school refusal might be serving. Interventions effectively addressing the specific purpose of school refusal with one type of child may be inappropriate or ineffective with a child whose school refusal is motivated by another purpose.

Chapter Seven

School Refusal for Avoidance of Stimuli That Provoke a Sense of General Negative Affect (SPNA)

Kelley is a seven year old child who is lying in the middle of the kitchen floor on Sunday night curled up in a fetal position and moaning about how " bad she feels." She wakes up every school morning complaining about how she aches all over, feels like she is going to throw up, and has a headache. Several visits to the pediatrician in the past month have found nothing to indicate any significant organic basis for her complaints. She resists getting out of bed, dawdles, and has to be reminded constantly to complete the next task of getting ready for school. She is resistive to attempts to help her get ready for school and the closer it gets to time to leave for school, the more generally resistive and distraught she becomes.

Kelley reports not wanting to go to school for fear that something bad will happen and states: "whenever I'm at school I feel yucky all the time." When asked why she doesn't want to go to school, she cannot give a logical reason except, "I feel horrible when I'm there." She complains that whenever she goes to school she feels sad and can't help herself and sometimes just starts to "cry for no reason." She knows that most kids don't really like to go to school, but for her it's just "awful and worse than it is for others." She pleads with her parents to let her go to another school despite the fact that all her brothers and sisters attend the same school quite willingly. In fact Kelly had no problem attending the school for kindergarten and first grade. Her parents are not willing to move her to another school, but in frustration are considering home-schooling "until she can get over the hump."

Treatment Components for Youth with Anxiety Based Avoidance of Stimuli That Provoke Negative Affectivity: (SPNA) School Refusal

Children who are refusing school to avoid the stimuli associated with school (SPNA) and the accompanying anxiety levels or state of general negative affectivity are motivated by discomfort. They will engage in behaviors to escape school or avoid it entirely. Interventions must attempt to alleviate the current state of distress, identify the aspect of the stimulus which is producing the negative affect, and create changes at a cognitive, affective, and behavioral level.

Pharmacotherapy

Early treatment of school refusal typically involved a medical and pharmacological approach, as pediatricians and family care practitioners often served as the initial intervention agents. Children often developed inappropriate escape strategies by feigning physical symptoms or may have misinterpreted the physiological components of their anxiety as physical disorders or illnesses. For parents who had a child complaining about physical ailments, the physician or pediatrician was normally consulted first. Once physiological issues and an organic basis for the symptoms were ruled out, the assumption was made that the physical symptoms and accompanying school refusal were fear or anxiety based. In many instances the treatments involved using antidepressants or anxiolytics.

During the 1970's and 1980's there was significant support for using imipramine (tofranil), but is currently considered off label for use with children other than for treatment of enuresis. Generally, the use of any medication is probably best avoided in treating school refusal, unless there are extremely high anxiety levels, school refusal is comorbid with major psychological disorders (Obsessive Compulsive Disorder, Oppositional Defiant Disorder, or Major Depressive Disorder) requiring psychotropic medications, or the child has been unresponsive to psychological treatment for school refusal in the past. If medications are to be utilized it is advantageous to use them in accompaniment with psychotherapy (Berg, 1997).

In a recent article, Tyrrell (2005) stated that "youth with anxiety based absenteeism respond ambiguously to medications, in part because of the fluid and amorphous nature of anxiety and depressive symptoms in this population." Kearney (2006a) reported that the use of SSRI's has been found useful in youth with anxiety and depression with comorbid school refusal. Kearney (2007a) stated that several studies have shown that medications can be effective with children with high levels of distress as the medications ease the "physical feelings" of anxiety. He cautioned that the medications may ease the "physical feelings" of distress without changing the cognitive or behavioral aspects of the distress. The child may physically feel better, but may still have thoughts about not wanting to attend or continuing to refuse to attend school.

If pharmacological intervention is to be utilized, it is most likely to be effective with the child who is overwhelmed by the emotional distress of attending school. However,

70

medication should be reserved for those children suffering with significant distress from underlying anxiety and depression and not the situational variables of school refusal (Kearney, 2007a). Utilizing medication for treating the underlying anxiety and depression may bring about relief for the school refusal indirectly, but it would be hard to state that any medication is effective in treating school refusal behaviors, particularly non-anxiety based school refusal. It should also be noted that the most effective treatment for anxiety and depression is a combination of medication and therapy.

For those children who have been on medication for anxiety and depression for a significant time and whose school refusal continues to be problematic, it may be necessary to modify the medication regimen and introduce ongoing psychotherapy to achieve a level of relief which allows the child to attend school. Other children may have been in therapy for a significant length of time, treating their anxiety or depression, and yet continue to experience significant distress when it comes to attending school. For those children, actively in treatment, whose school refusal behaviors continue to persist and who are unresponsive to other interventions, the introduction of an appropriate medication regimen to treat their anxiety and depression may be required. In either case, parents, school personnel, and mental health professionals should be clear that the medication is being utilized to deal with the underlying anxiety and depression and not as a primary treatment for school refusal.

Cognitive-Behavioral Therapy

School refusal behavior for many children and adolescents can be highly anxiety and depression based. Until interventions appropriately address any underlying or comorbid anxiety and/or depression, it is unlikely that school refusing behaviors will change significantly. Classical cognitive-behavioral techniques have been demonstrated to be very effective at intervening with this population (King et al., 1998, Last, Hansen, & Franco, 1998, and Wimmer, 2003). Cognitive elements have typically involved attempting to assist the child in recognizing and identifying anxious feelings and the somatic indicators of anxiety which they may experience as it relates to attending school. Walking a child through the process of clarifying unrealistic or negative expectations and anxiety provoking thoughts may be helpful in identifying the cognitive distortions which the child may be experiencing. However, in many instances, the child may lack the capacity for self-reflection and may not be able to identify specific aspects of the school experience which are anxiety provoking. In these cases, the explanation may be limited to: "I don't know," or "school just makes me feel bad."

If the child can assist in identifying some of the cognitions and cognitive distortions, the therapist or school counselor may be of great assistance in helping the child to develop appropriate coping strategies. In those situations, positive self-talk, breathing, relaxation, distractions, etc. are very effective at reducing school refusal. A variety of options may be attempted to develop more appropriate coping strategies other than simply refusing to attend school. A plan of action and intervention can be developed to insure an understanding of the various coping behaviors. Plans for self-reinforcement through new cognitions may produce less anxiety and discomfort.

Once cognitive components have been analyzed and identified, behavioral changes can be attempted which will lead to a more normalized response to the stimuli of school attendance. Guided imagery or visualization of school attendance can be utilized to pair new somatic feelings and evaluations with the behavior of school attendance. Utilizing *in vivo* exposure by gradually exposing the child to the stimuli of the school experience may allow for desensitization to the stimuli of school attendance. This can be accomplished through gradual, stepwise exposure to the school building, hallways, and classrooms or through gradually exposing the child to longer and longer periods of time in the school setting (King et al., 2000).

Many particularly anxious and fear based school refusers can be overwhelmed with their anxiety due to the complexity and ambiguity of the school situation and not having an adequate experience base for attending school. Providing a model, such as an older sibling or "a buddy," in the form of another child who is comfortable with attending school can be an effective means of handling the situation. Creating a fantasy or role playing situation where the child can create their own scenarios with appropriate coaching may also be effective at lowering overall anxiety. Exercises which provide the child some sense of control over their somatic and affective experiences, such as deep breathing or muscle relaxation training, may provide enough comfort that the child can cope with the discomfort produced by the stimuli of school attendance.

Kearney and Albano (2007) and Kearney (2008a) have suggested that for this particular function of school refusal (SPNA), the most effective strategy is leading the child through the process of identifying the "feeling, thinking, and doing" of school refusal. First, assist the child in identifying their feelings, sweaty palms, queasy stomach, shaking hand, rapid heartbeat, etc. and labeling those as things I feel. Second, assist the child in identifying their thoughts and what they are saying to themselves, thoughts like "I've got to get out of here," "I'm afraid," "I want to go home," "I need my mom or someone to help me." Finally, assist the child in identifying what they usually do in the situation of having to attend school, such as leaving the room, going to the counselor's or nurse's office, crying, or throwing a tantrum.

Once you have identified the affect, cognitions, and behaviors, modifying thoughts to be more appropriate and realistic through self talk, understanding the nature of their feelings and that anxiety is the body's way of preparing them to respond, and changing some of the self-defeating behavior patterns can be accomplished. Breathing, muscle relaxation, defocusing, and self-distraction can be effective ways of managing the "feeling" part of their distress. In many situations, changing the "thinking" or self-talk is most effectively addressed by providing more positive and realistic thought patterns. Parents and school personnel should avoid truisms such as "There's nothing to be afraid of," "Suck it up and be a man," "You're not really afraid," or other statements which do not acknowledge the reality of their discomfort.

Reframing their discomfort, by acknowledging whatever realistic component may be there and then normalizing it to make it more acceptable, temporary, transitional, and optimistic is probably a more realistic strategy. Finally working with the "doing" part of the school refusal may require the parent and school personnel to tolerate some behaviors on a temporary basis. Modifying the length, duration, and intensity of school refusing behaviors, while moving toward a goal of complete removal of school refusal behaviors and a full return to school,

74

may have to be accepted as progress. Attending for part of the day, attending for favorite classes, limiting visits to the counselor or nurse on a declining scale, or leaving the room for shorter time periods may be effective as a first step to modifying some of the school refusal behaviors.

Psychoeducation

For some children, the experience of attending school is often their first major experience of anxiety which they cannot avoid or escape. The experience of anxiety with the accompanying somatic changes and affective discomfort may be overwhelming and may be misinterpreted as a life threatening experience. In many situations, the counselor can provide a child with an understanding of what is happening to them and reassure them that anxiety is not life threatening, but a normal component of daily living. The counselor's role may be to educate the youth regarding the nature of feelings, negative thoughts, somatic aspects, and negative behaviors which comprise anxiety.

The counselor can also educate the child that attempting to go through life without ever experiencing anxiety is an impossible goal. Living necessarily implies that, from time to time, we will experience the negative physical, emotional, and behavioral components which accompany anxiety. The counselor's role in these situations is to teach the child to self-monitor and distinguish the nature and severity of anxiety. The counselor may also introduce the concept of gradual exposure to anxiety and attaining a level of relative comfort, with the ultimate goal of full attendance with manageable anxiety. The youth may benefit in other ways by being empowered to cope with the normal levels of anxiety which come with functioning in an age appropriate fashion.

Build a Negative Affective-Avoidance Hierarchy

Another effective method for assisting the child in managing their anxiety about school attendance is building a hierarchy of anxiety provoking situations (Kearney, 2001 and Kearney & Albano, 2007). Working through a hierarchy and assigning a specific strength to the anxiety and fear associated with particular aspects of school attendance allows the child to compartmentalize the problem and identify those aspects which produce the greatest discomfort. The child is an active participant in identifying the level of distress and is forced to move away from a more generalized fear response. The sorting and rating process also allows the counselor to assist the child in understanding the difference between a "fear" and an activity which does not produce a fear response, but one which is undesirable and which the child would prefer to avoid if possible.

The child can be assisted in identifying what aspects of school attendance produce such an overwhelming fear response that they just "can't" attend, right now, versus those aspects of school attendance which do not produce fear, but which the child just "won't" attend because the stimuli are unpleasant or undesirable. At that point, behavioral objectives can be established to complete some of the undesirable or avoidance behaviors. Simultaneously, the child and counselor can continue to work on developing the coping skills necessary to do some of the steps which the child feels that she "can't" do without extreme fear.

Somatic Control Exercises

Providing the child with the experience and awareness of the fact that they can actively control and alter the negative feelings they have when attending school will go a long way toward allowing the child to endure the discomfort of school attendance. Stress reduction exercises such as squeezing and releasing a "tension ball," tearing paper into strips, diaphragmatic breathing, etc. all give the child some sense of control over how they are feeling and reduce some of the "panic" of attending school. Muscle tension and relaxation techniques can also be very effective in reducing the anxiety and bodily tension which the child may be experiencing while attending school. Alternately tensing and releasing muscle groups can provide an active strategy that the child can employ to manage his or her anxiety. The "Robot-Rag Doll" (Kendall et al, 1992) technique of tensing all the muscles in your body and holding it for 10 seconds and then releasing the tension by becoming a rag doll is very effective with younger children.

Formalized desensitization, either imaginal or *in vivo*, provides another way of managing the physical discomfort accompanying the anxiety of school attendance. Desensitization through the use of guided imagery (sights, sounds, smells, feelings, places, and thoughts) is an effective starting point for a child who refuses school as a result of the anxiety which the stimuli of school produces for them. Asking the child to imagine a pleasurable image or scene in great detail until their discomfort level is negligible and then asking them to begin to imagine various aspects of the stimuli of going to school and to rate their level of discomfort on a scale of 1 to 100. When images of school attendance reach a discomfort level above 50, introduce breathing, relaxation techniques, or a return to the pleasurable scene until they can return to a tolerable discomfort level. Processing with the child the activity and empowering them to utilize these techniques when they become anxious in school can be an effective intervention.

A similar approach can be to desensitize the child to the stimuli of school attendance by utilizing an *in vivo approach.* Gradual exposure to the school building, with a similar rating of discomfort, and intervening with breathing, muscle relaxation, habituation, or pleasurable images or fantasy can recondition the child to respond to the stimuli of school attendance in a different fashion. Gradual exposure to elements of a real school setting (the bus, office, classroom, teacher, etc.) and pairing those stimuli with a relaxation response will create a new stimulus-response contingency. Some children may be able to attend school, but only with an inappropriate coping strategy such as sucking their thumb, having a parent in the room, bringing a stuffed animal, etc. Gradual removal of *safety objects* or stimuli can be achieved in a similar fashion utilizing desensitization techniques.

The following case study will provide an opportunity to develop an individualized strategic intervention plan as discussed earlier. After the case description, there is a template which will facilitate the development of an intervention plan based on 1) identifying the purpose which the school refusal serves, 2) identifying and underlying or comorbid conditions, 3) establishing intervention goals, and 4) developing tentative objectives to achieve those goals. Sample answers are provided in Appendix A.

78

"School Makes Me Want to Throw Up"

Eric Eggplant is an eight year old boy who had recently transferred to a new school. For the first three weeks of third grade he had spent only part of the day at school either curled up in a ball on his classroom floor or trying to run from the school building. His mother reports that the behavior started at the end of last year and attributed it to his teacher being a "witch." At the end of the year his mother sought to have him transferred out of the" school that had no feelings." Eric would awaken each morning with a stomach ache and then proceed to vomit. On days when he did not vomit or his mother made him go to school he would fight her in the car or vomit in the parking lot. When asked what the teacher did that was so mean, Eric could not give any examples. He stated that his teacher this year is not mean, the kids are not mean, and he can think of no reasons why he can't stay at school all day, other than school "makes me want to throw up."

Eric's mother acknowledged that there had been some difficulty getting him to go to school in kindergarten, but it quickly faded. She attributed much of this to the teacher "who was an angel." His mother has tried talking to him, "bribing" him, and punishing him, and refusing to come to school when Eric called complaining about being sick. The last episode where he ran from the building caused a great deal of alarm among his mother and the school administration.

This year has been particularly difficult for Eric as a result of his parents' separation. Divorce papers were filed but ultimately withdrawn as his parents try to work things out. Eric still wants his father to come home and live with them and doesn't understand why he won't just move back in. He has been

79

experiencing frequent nightmares and has suddenly developed an extreme fear of thunder and lightning. He will no longer sleep in a dark room and many nights, ends up in bed with his mother simply "because it's easier." He has also regressed to wetting the bed and refuses to do things by himself which his mother knows he can do.

Type of School Refusal___*Avoidance of Stimuli that Provoke A Sense of General Negative Affect (SPNA)*

Underlying or Comorbid
Conditions_____

_____

_____

Goal
A_____

_____

Objective1_____

_____

Objective2_____

_____

Objective3_____

_____

Goal
B_____

_____

Objective1_____

_____

Objective2_____

_____

Objective3_____

_____

Goal C_____

_____

Objective1_____

_____

Objective2_____

_____

Objective3_____

_____

Goal D_____

_____

Objective1_____

_____

Objective2_____

_____

Objective3_____

_____

Chapter Eight

School Refusal to Escape from Aversive Social or Evaluative Situations (EASE)

Joseph is a fourteen year old boy who has just started his freshman year in high school and has started resisting going to school. He reports being particularly nervous in classes where he has to perform in front of the class or do "group work." He has begun leaving school without permission after attending some morning classes. Joseph reports that he doesn't feel like he fits in at school and is frequently ridiculed by other students, particularly the "jocks," who see Joseph as weird and unmanly. Since he started high school three months ago, he has been a target of ridicule on Facebook and has had videos which other students made of him posted on YouTube.

Joseph came from a small middle school where the staff and students were more accepting of Joseph's "weird statements" and his manner of dressing in very baggy and worn clothes due to his sensitivity to certain fabrics. In his old school he had one or two "friends" but recently it has been reported that he talks to none of the students and is only verbal as required with staff members. Joseph has become more resistive about going to school as "I get nothing out of it, and I already know everything they can teach me." He has been requesting that his parents allow him to withdraw and take his high school courses through e-school.

Treatment Components for Youth Who Escape Aversive Social or Evaluative Situations: (EASE) School Refusal

For these children, the place where they experience humiliation, ridicule, rejection, debasement, shame, and being devalued is in the context of attending school. The child who is refusing school to escape from the Aversive Social and Evaluative Situations (EASE) which come with attending school will engage in behaviors to escape school or avoid school entirely. Intervention will need to attempt to alleviate the unpleasant social and evaluative components of school attendance through changing social cognitions, providing social skills, creating the opportunities for social and academic success, and gradual exposure to normal social situations.

Cognitive-Behavioral Therapy

Kearney and Albano (2000, 2007) and Kearney (2008a) have proposed the same kind of "thinking," "feeling," and "doing" approach for dealing with school refusal which has at its core social anxiety and the fear of "measuring up" in certain situations. The particular dysfunctional escape behaviors, which these youth may engage in to avoid the social and evaluative components of school, can be displayed in a variety of ways. These might include walking the hallways without speaking or making eye contact, hiding in the library or restroom during pep rallies or other group gatherings, avoiding interactions with other students or staff members, refusing to participate actively in group discussions or "group projects," and avoiding or becoming ill when it is their turn to present in class or take a test.

These children who are refusing school may be attempting to escape from an aversive situation which actually has very little to do with the actual school or school setting. Their anxiety about attending school derives from the fact that school is a social setting requiring their interaction with peers and school personnel. The social anxiety produced by the exposure to other children and unknown adults is often a sufficient cause to avoid or refuse attending school. The social anxiety may stem from both a biological predisposition toward anxiety as well as faulty cognitions and faulty self perceptions about social interaction in general, and school in particular. Until the social anxiety and fear of criticism or ridicule has been resolved it is very unlikely that these children will be able to attend school without considerable anxiety or significant escape and avoidance behaviors. This social anxiety and sensitivity to evaluation or criticism is best dealt with by a cognitive/behavioral approach (Kearney & Albano, 2007).

Children who avoid or refuse to attend school due to the social nature of the experience (EASE) have many cognitive distortions about social interactions in general. The unstructured nature of the social exchange which takes place during a typical school day may be particularly anxiety provoking. These youth may be overly sensitive to slights or comments and have a cognitive frame which is rampant with distortions. Their belief, that they are socially incompetent or that other children are "out to get them," results in a negative frame which may become a self-fulfilling prophesy. Many of these youth anticipate social rejection and either distort or misinterpret social stimuli or cues. They may lack the ability to accurately perceive or decode social situations in an appropriate fashion. Characteristically, these children lack effective communication skills and either over communicate or under communicate in social situations.

Changing their cognitions regarding the social aspects of school attendance may be very difficult, as these children often have had limited success with social interactions and view themselves as "shy," "socially awkward," or "just different." Many may be unskilled or inexperienced at handling even simple social situations, conflicts, or interactions. Providing training in social problem solving through a social skills group can alleviate some of the anxiety by providing them some sense of competence and social success. Working with the school counselor to brainstorm hypothetical social situations which they might experience at school provides them the time to think through the situation, rather than have to improvise behavior for every new situation. Having a counselor pose "hypothetical" social interaction situations and walking the youth through possible responses, identifying the positives and negatives associated with each alternative, can also be helpful in providing a sense of social competence through prior exposure.

Role playing potential social interactions in counseling may also be effective at reducing the discomfort which these youth experience in the social and evaluative context of school. Providing them the opportunity to practice various responses in session, receiving feedback on how they handled the situation, and ways to improve their comfort in social settings can be very reassuring. Additional specific training at identifying and interpreting facial cues, body language, and other non-verbal aspects of human interaction and communication can also be very helpful at resolving the social anxiety which accompanies school attendance.

Psychoeducation

Another potential intervention for this particular group of school refusers is to provide them with information about the nature of social anxiety. This can be accomplished by educating the youth regarding the nature of feelings, negative thoughts, somatic concerns, physical symptoms, and negative behaviors which comprise social anxiety. Providing them with an alternative frame of reference regarding the feelings they experience in social settings can be very helpful. The child can be helped to understand that the goal is not to avoid or limit the experience of social anxiety, but to be capable of reading and understanding what their body is telling them. Totally eliminating social anxiety from their life is unrealistic and may actually be counterproductive toward developing a healthy psychological adjustment.

Teaching the child to distinguish between "normal" social anxiety and severe social anxiety is a key component to ending the debilitation which these children experience. This can be accomplished by introducing the concept of gradual exposure to social anxiety provoking situations and the concepts of regression to the mean, habituation, and "fading" as a result of acclimation. Pushing themselves to attend school and deal with a relatively uncomfortable level of anxiety for a brief period may allow them to eventually attend in a fairly normal pattern with a fairly normal level of anxiety.

An effective tool toward normalizing social anxiety is helping the youth build a Social/Evaluative Anxiety versus Avoidance Hierarchy (Kearney, 2007a and Kearney & Albano, 2007). For some children the social/evaluative anxiety may be so severe that they cannot deal with a particular situation, at this time. Other stimuli produce much less social/evaluative anxiety, but are still undesirable and are avoided whenever possible. Chronic avoidance behaviors result in severe limitations in the ability to function in a psychologically and socially typical fashion. Assisting the child with a sorting process which distinguishes what is an overwhelming feeling of anxiety and what is avoidance begins to identify the aspects of the school refusal that truly are a "can't, at this time" versus those that are a "won't, because it's uncomfortable or difficult." The child rates various social/evaluative components of school attendance by placing them on a social fear thermometer (rate from 1 to 100) and a discomfort or dislike level to clarify the stimulus value. Establishing the level of distress and level of avoidance for a variety of social or evaluative situations in the school setting may allow the counselor to develop interventions on lower value stimuli. This guarantees some movement on the school refusal behavior issue by a modification of the stimuli or reframing of the stimuli. The goal is to ultimately move the stimuli to a level which is acceptable to the child.

Cognitive Restructuring

In many instances the youth may have created a series of social and evaluative cognitive distortions around attending school which make it difficult if not impossible for him or her to attend. Many children may catastrophize situations involving a social and evaluative component to a level that they are no longer comfortable or capable of attending school. The negative cognitions about attending school are so extreme that a safer recourse is to limit the danger by avoiding or refusing school attendance completely. Normal missteps in social functioning become disastrous public humiliations which are to be avoided at all costs. Failure to achieve at a certain level becomes an absolute confirmation of their incompetence and deficiency. For many these social cognitions become a self-fulfilling prophesy leading to further school refusal.

Negative thinking leads to poor performance. If the child thinks that they are socially incompetent, they will very likely behave in a socially incompetent fashion. Their negative perception, that they are socially incompetent and their internal thought process, will create an interaction which is stiff and formal or awkward and bizarre, thereby decreasing the comfort level of the other participant in the social interaction. The other participant's discomfort with this abnormal interaction pattern is likely to make them react, reject or avoid interaction with a child who feels uncomfortable interacting socially. The child's awareness of the discomfort their interaction creates in the other participant makes them even less capable or interacting in a relaxed fashion, and the cycle continues to deteriorate. Their social interactions may need to be experienced in a more productive and fruitful fashion, which allows them to feel comfortable and successful in the social aspects of attending school. The counselor can assist in training the child to restructure their thinking and feeling reactions by using simple anagrams to reflect on their experience and change their thinking, feeling, and behavioral patterns such as **FEAR** (Kendall, et. al.1992) or **STOP** (Silverman & Kurtines, 1996).

- **FEAR - F** what am I *feeling*, **E** what do I *expect*, **A** what *actions* and *attitudes* will help, and **R** what might be the *results* or *rewards*
- **STOP - S** are you *scared*, **T** what are you *thinking*, **O** what *other* thoughts and behaviors can you think of, and **P** *praise* yourself and *plan* for the future
- With older children you can use more traditional cognitive-behavior therapy (Beck, 1979) and focus on automatic thoughts, all-or-none thinking, catastrophizing, negative labeling, *"can't, should,* and *won't,"* and mindreading.

Behavioral Exposures

Once the counselor has developed a hierarchy of social anxiety stimuli in the school setting, lower level anxiety producing situations in the hierarchy can be targeted to gradual behavioral exposures. No matter how complex social anxiety may be, the situation and stimuli can be broken down into smaller simpler steps and specific stimuli. In every social situation, at a minimum there must be the recognition that someone else is a part of the situation and stimuli. This recognition may be as simple as making eye contact with another person or a verbal acknowledgment of the other person. Working on a simple behavior such as increased eye contact and habituating to the discomfort of making eye contact can be a first step to overcoming social anxiety. Using relaxation and self-talk techniques while attempting to perform lower level anxiety producing social interactions can assist the youth to overcome some of their anxiety about social or evaluative situations and progress to the next level of anxiety producing interaction.

Rehearsing social situations, which a youth is likely to encounter in the school setting, with a group of accepting peers can minimize the embarrassment factor and provide behavioral alternatives for handling difficult situations. Arming the child with a set of "conversation starter questions," allowing them to practice with adults or peers they feel comfortable with, and then attempting to start a conversation with an individual and then a small group can be a strategy for behavioral exposure in a gradual controlled fashion. Breaking down the behaviors which are anxiety provoking into social tasks which are specific, concrete, time limited, and measurable may increase the social confidence of the child to a level where they can attend school with a normal level of social anxiety.

The following case study will provide an opportunity to develop an individualized strategic intervention plan as discussed earlier. After the case description, there is a template which will facilitate the development of an intervention plan based on 1) identifying the purpose which the school refusal serves, 2) identifying and underlying or comorbid conditions, 3) establishing intervention goals, and 4) developing tentative objectives to achieve those goals. Sample answers are provided in Appendix A.

"Everybody There Hates Me"

Nicholas Noodle is fourteen and has just started his freshman year at a large county consolidated high school. The elementary and junior high he attended was in a small rural mining town. Since the beginning of school he has missed twenty-three days in the first quarter. Nicholas has stated that he hates the school, hates the kids, and hates the teachers, but cannot provide any concrete examples or reasons as to why he has such negative feelings. His response to discussing the situation is frequently, "everybody there hates me." He says the kids there are not like him and go out of their way to make remarks or make fun of him and his accent. He wishes the "old high school" had never been closed and consolidated with the school in the city.

When Nicholas is at school he often shows up late for first period which enables him to avoid hanging out in the halls with the other kids. He is often found eating his lunch by himself in the library rather than going to the cafeteria. Given a choice, he sits quietly in the back of class, never raises his hand to answer a question, goes mute when called on for an answer, and has real difficulty working in small groups. He often is "sick" on days where a test is scheduled and refuses to make up the test at school and would rather take a zero. Nicholas reports that he doesn't know any of the names of his new classmates and he has not made any friends since the start of school. If he talks to anyone it is the few kids who are from his old junior high school, but even with them he often just stands on the edge of the group and does not participate in the conversation.

When he stays home from school, he spends most of the day watching TV or playing video games. He is willing to do the make-up work or homework, which he completes quickly and accurately. He takes the initiative to go on line and download the class work and homework assignments and they are always completed by the time his parents get home. Recently, to everyone's surprise, Nicholas "cut" school, hitch-hiked home, and spent the day doing his class work and homework. Despite being punished, he has continued to leave the school without permission, but always goes straight home, despite the five mile walk. Other than cutting school, his parents report that Nicholas is not a problem and they describe him as a quiet, respectful, and compliant child. He seldom gets in trouble at home and is generally very helpful with the younger siblings. His parents are exploring the option of homebound instruction or allowing him to complete his classes online.

Type of School Refusal___ *Escape from Aversive Social or Evaluative Situations (EASE)*

Underlying or Comorbid Conditions

_____
_____
_____

Goal
A_____
_____

Objective1_____
_____

Objective2_____
_____

Objective3_____
_____

Goal
B_____
_____

Objective1_____
_____

Objective2_____
_____

Objective3_____
_____

Goal C_____

_____

Objective1_____

_____

Objective2_____

_____

Objective3_____

_____

Goal D_____

_____

Objective1_____

_____

Objective2_____

_____

Objective3_____

_____

Chapter Nine

School Refusal for Attention Seeking Behavior (AS)

Sam is an eight year old boy who has trouble attending school because he would much rather remain at home with his father than go to school. Since Dad has been recently laid off from work, Sam has started to beg and plead to stay at home with his Dad. When his father is successful in getting him to go to school, Sam obsesses all day long wondering if his father will be waiting for him at the bus stop when he gets out of school. Sam begs and pleads with the office staff and his teacher to allow him to call home to "check on his Dad." On days when his father is able to get him to go to school, there is typically a tearful scene in the parking lot or Sam refuses to get out of the car. Sam has threatened to hang himself with the car seat belt if his father makes him go in. Sam has also engaged in a great deal of drama on school mornings with lots of tears, screaming, and being generally disruptive and disobedient. Punishment for these behaviors has been unsuccessful. On at least two occasions Sam has hidden the car keys and refused to tell his father where they were.

On at least two occasions, Sam has actually left the school grounds and walked home when he knew that his father was at home. When he does get to school and remains for the day, Sam obsesses about his father and wonders what he is doing at home. His academic work is suffering now as he is not organized and is having difficulty concentrating and focusing. Sam is very happy and content at home and on the weekends and even volunteers for "work projects" as long as he can be with his father. Sam continually begs and pleads with his parents to withdraw him from school and allow his father to home-school him "since he's there anyway." Short of that, Sam's solution is to allow his father to come to school with him and be the volunteer aide in the classroom.

Treatment Components for Youth Who Refuse School for Attention: (ASB) School Refusal

For some youth, the purpose of their school refusal behavior is less about avoiding attendance at school and more a product of a desire for attention and recognition. Having an issue with attending school can be a very powerful way for the child to rally the adults in their life to provide a great deal of care and concern. In many instances, parents and school personnel may be inadvertently reinforcing the undesired school refusal by becoming overly involved or overly concerned. Much of the intervention in these situations involves assisting the parents and school personnel to restructure the reinforcement contingencies in a more appropriate fashion.

Restructuring Parent Commands

Parents are understandably concerned about their child's inability or unwillingness to attend school. The interaction pattern of the parent and the child may be reinforcing non-attendance and in some instances the parent may actually be a co-collaborator or co-conspirator in the child's school refusal. Perhaps unintentionally or unconsciously, the parents may be interacting with the child in a fashion which actually reinforces school refusal behavior. It is very likely that parents have discussed, begged, pleaded, cajoled, or even threatened the child with severe consequences around the issue of the school refusal. In many instances what the parents are saying to the child is much less important than the reward value of having the parent's complete attention and the child being in control of the situation. Typically, for the child whose school refusal is about attention, no amount of lecturing, discussion, or promises of rewards or consequences will be sufficient to change the behavior since the real reinforcement is the interaction between the child and parent or child and teacher (Kearney, 2001).

Many parents may mistakenly feel that they can control the situation and the school refusal through their verbal interaction with the child and resort to pleading, criticism, shame, sarcasm, ridicule, excessive support, understanding, or lecturing. The counselor's role in these situations is to assist the parents and authority figures in transforming long debates/discussions/pleadings into short commands and simple child responses. Educating parents to be parental, and giving them permission to act as authoritative figures may also be critical to managing the school refusal behavior.. Assisting parents in learning how to identify key errors in parental commands: commands that are **question like** (Do you think you'll be able to go to school today?), **vague** (It's 7:30), **incomplete** (find your backpack), or **multi-step or excessively long** (get your backpack, empty the dishwasher, help your brother, get to the bus stop, and help me find your library books) almost insure non-compliance.

Issuing direct simple commands which move the child toward behaviors resulting in attendance at school are the most effective. Many school refusers realize that passivity is their greatest weapon in increasing the likelihood that they won't be required to attend school. It also increases the likelihood that the child will receive attention, albeit negative attention. Parents should be coached with how to deal with passivity in a non-attending, non-reinforcing fashion and always be prepared with an option for non-compliance to any parental command (Heyne & Rollings, 2006).

Ignoring Simple Inappropriate Behaviors

Since the purpose of the school refusal for these children is to obtain attention and connection to parents, any activity seeking compliance which reinforces inappropriate behavior should be avoided. Lecturing, yelling, negotiating, trying to calm, or physical force are inappropriate for intervening with attention seekers, as these behaviors only serve to reinforce the unacceptable behavior. Whenever possible, ignore inappropriate behaviors. The counselor's role may be to teach parents to avoid reinforcing inappropriate behavior through averting eye contact, "going silent," looking over the child or through them, administering a "time out," isolating the child from attention and interaction, or attending to siblings and other activities (Kearney and Albano, 2007).

Parents may have to develop a capacity to ignore physical complaints which are not grounded in some demonstrable symptom. Utilizing the criteria of the three **B's**, "if you are not **burning, bleeding or broken** you must attend school" provides a way of avoiding the endless debates over psychosomatic physical symptoms. In those situations where the child is legitimately sick, the counselor can encourage parents to show little physical or verbal attention and the child must remain in bed during school hours to avoid reinforcing being sick as a way of avoiding school.

Establish Fixed Routines

The child who is seeking attention through his or her school refusal (ASB) may engage in a variety of escape and avoidance behaviors which are extremely disruptive and frustrating. Creating chaos, or a scene every morning, is doubly reinforcing as it requires attention from the parents and if successful prevents the child from attending school. Encouraging parents to develop a rigid morning routine, which does not vary and cannot be derailed by the child's disruptive behaviors, will be very important in insuring that the child makes it to school in the morning. Requiring the child to awaken 90 – 120 minutes before the start of school provides a "cushion" to deal with the disruptive behaviors.

The counselor can also be of assistance by reframing the parent's concern about being tardy or late into it's important to get the child her no matter what time they arrive. Encouraging parents to insure that the message the child receives is "you will eventually be required to go to school no matter how much you delay or are disruptive" is a key toward changing the child's response pattern. If the parent is absolutely unable to require the child to attend, daytime contact with the child should be limited, and the evening should focus on completing homework and "serving time for missing school" with an absolute minimal contact with the parent. Establishing a point system for behaviors necessary for school attendance with appropriate consequences and rewards may be an effective way to change the response patterns and the parent child dynamics.

Excessive Reassurance Seeking Behavior

Another delay or avoidance tactic utilized by many of these children (ASB) is repeatedly and excessively asking for reassurance. This serves as a dual reward system, as it galvanizes the parent's need to respond to their child by giving them attention by answering repetitive questions, and if exercised sufficiently may delay or prevent the child from attending school. Frequently the child may ask the same question, or make the same plea, over and over in a never ending stream of "what ifs." This requires the parent to continue to interact with the child and avoid the possibility of actually going to school in a timely fashion. Parents should be encouraged to answer the question once; on the second attempt remind the child that she knows the answer; and then ignore all subsequent attempts to ask another version of the question.

In a similar vein, the child at school may also request frequent calls home to seek reassurance. These behaviors should be placed on a diminishing reinforcement schedule. Calls in excess are grounds for punishment that night. Days without calls home should be reinforced with an appropriate recognition and reward. Rewarding a "call free day" with one-on-one attention allows the child to fill their need for attention through appropriate behaviors rather than inappropriate methods for seeking attention and a connection to the parent (Kearney, 2001).

The following case study will provide an opportunity to develop an individualized strategic intervention plan as discussed earlier. After the case description, there is a template which will facilitate the development of an intervention plan based on 1) identifying the purpose which the school refusal serves, 2) identifying and underlying or comorbid conditions, 3) establishing intervention goals, and 4) developing tentative objectives to achieve those goals. Sample answers are provided in Appendix A.

"Can't I Stay at Home and Have You Teach Me"

Rebecca Rigatoni, *an eight year old girl, has always had difficulty attending school, but has attended with much coaxing and encouragement until she started the third grade. Since then the problem has worsened significantly. She begs to stay home from school and when her pleading does not work she resorts to screaming, being oppositional, and resisting getting dressed which often results in her missing the bus. Rebecca insists that she doesn't want to go to school because it makes her feel sad and afraid. She cannot identify anything or anyone at school that makes her fearful and insists her teacher and the other students are "nice." Her mom is frequently required to bring her to school in the family car and Rebecca has piled up a number of tardies. Rebecca knows her mother is a former teacher and she wants to stay home and have her mother teach her what she needs to know.*

Upon arriving at school, Rebecca frequently begins complaining that she is sick and asks to go to the office. She is on a first name basis with the office staff and attempts to get them to call her mother to pick her up. Sometimes simply talking to her mother will allow her to return to class. If she is sent back to her classroom, she frequently returns to the office during the next period. Her mother usually resorts to picking her up at least twice a week. When she gets home she usually spends the time in the presence of her mother playing quietly or watching TV. Rebecca's solution to the problem is for her mother to get her a cell phone which she can take to school. This is a violation of school policy. Her teacher indicates that Rebecca is a good student, and somehow manages to keep up academically, despite her frequent absences. She is cooperative and pleasant unless the teacher refuses to let Rebecca go to the office and then she can become quite difficult and tearful.

Mrs. Rigatoni reports that Rebecca often tells her that she would rather be at home than go to school and when she is at school all she can think about is her mother and baby brother. Mrs. Rigatoni had taught school prior to the birth of her children and Rebecca has often insisted that she could teach Rebecca at home. Rebecca has a number of friends in the neighborhood, but gets into moods where she won't leave the house and follows her mother from room to room.

Type of School Refusal___ *Attention Seeking*
Behavior(ASB)

Underlying or Comorbid Conditions

_____
_____

Goal
A_____
_____

Objective1_____
_____

Objective2_____
_____

Objective3_____
_____

Goal
B_____
_____

Objective1_____
_____

Objective2_____
_____

Objective3_____
_____

**Goal
C**_____

_____

Objective1_____

_____

Objective2_____

_____

Objective3_____

_____

**Goal
D**_____

_____

Objective1_____

_____

Objective2_____

_____

Objective3_____

_____

Chapter Ten

School Refusal for Tangible Reinforcers Outside of School (TROS)

Maya is a sixteen-year-old female in her junior year at a local high school. Maya has had no real attendance problems up until this year when she began hanging out with a new group of friends. She most typically comes to school in the morning "to see her friends." She reports that school has nothing to offer her and all day long "they make me do boring stuff." Her friends often encourage her to "cut" class and go to the local mall with them. As a result her grades are suffering.

Maya reports no particular distress about attending school, but doesn't see it as a particularly useful activity. She has even gotten other youth to get the assignments for her and occasionally she does them at home and then has someone turn the work in for her. As a result, her absence at school is not always noted and she continues to be places other than at school. When her parents challenge her absence at school, Maya actively insists that she was at school and " I can get four of my friends to swear I was there today." The school also has a number of written excuses for leaving school early which look very suspicious. Maya is very popular with her peers and is considered "the life of the party." On one of her absences, she was accused of shoplifting at the mall, and when her parents were called, they talked the store personnel out of filing charges. As a result of that incident she is "grounded for life" and her parents have taken away her cell phone and her ability to text her friends.

Treatment Components for Youth Who Refuse School for Tangible Reinforcement Outside School: (TROS) School Refusal

For this particular group of children (TROS), the school refusal is less anxiety or attention based and involves issues of controlling the environment and the demands made on them for school attendance (Kearney, 2008a). School attendance may not be a particularly rewarding experience for these youth and often other concrete reinforcers in the environment may be pursued rather than attending school. This struggle for control and for controlling the environment often leads to highly conflictual situations. Because antagonism, conflict, and poor problem solving are common to many of these families, the intervention goals typically involve enhancing the family's ability to resolve conflict around the school refusal effectively. The components of functionally based treatment for this group of school refusers includes: contracting, escorting the child to school, communication skills training, and peer refusal skills training.

Contracting for Attendance

Contracting for school attendance is typically a much more complex activity due to a number of factors. Many families have developed a dynamic of mutual distrust between the child and the parent. Both parties have presented "empty promises" in the past and an attitude of mutual distrust makes contracting for anything a highly suspicious and tenuous activity. By the

107

time the youth is capable of opting for more rewarding situations by refusing to attend school, the ability to require school attendance is minimal, at best, on the part of the parent.

Due to the level of conflict in these families, initial and subsequent contract negotiation may have to take place under supervision of a therapist or counselor working with the child and his family. In order to effectively contract with the youth, the first step may be to reestablish the belief that both the child and his parents are capable of effectively negotiating and honoring a contract. The first contract should involve an easily defined problem which has little to do with school attendance, such as chores, curfew, personal responsibility, etc. Kearney (2001) has suggested that for the first contract, simplicity is the key. Parents and youth should not attempt to tackle convoluted, complex, or volatile situations. Generating as many solutions as possible to a very concrete problem situation and trying to have all parties arrive at a consensus are keys. Once consensus is reached about solutions to the problem situation, the child and parent attempt to define rewards for compliance and consequences for non-compliance. The first contract should be 1) simple and straightforward, 2) last no longer than 2-3 weeks, 3) eliminate all loopholes or excuses, and 4) have exact definitions regarding timelines, responsibilities, and criteria for successful completion.

If parents and the youth can successfully negotiate and conform to the specifications of a simple contract, then an attempt at developing a contract for school attendance can be negotiated. The school attendance contract should only be attempted after a successful first contract and at a time when there is not severe conflict existing between parent and child. The contract may have to be stepwise and establish the beginning elements of a precursor to full attendance. Full attendance may need to be phased in initially to insure
108

compliance and increase the possibility of success. The contract should also require completion of school work at home and chores. Linking attendance at school with the most powerful positive reinforcer (extension of curfew, sleepovers, additional time with friends, shopping, video games, phone, computer, rides for friends, tattoos, use of family car, etc.) increases the likelihood of success. Parents may also wish to link attendance with the opportunity to earn money or additional privileges by completion of chores, contingent on attendance of school. The following is a sample of a typical school attendance contract:

School Attendance Contract

In exchange for decreased family tension and a resolution to the school problem, all family members agree to try as hard as possible to honor the contract.

In exchange for the privilege of being paid $25 for cutting the grass and feeding the dog, Bobby agrees to attend school each day from 10 to 2.

Should he not complete his responsibility for attending school, he will cut the grass and feed the dog without being paid.

Should he not complete these chores, the Game Cube will be removed for 1 week.

In exchange for the privilege of playing football, Bobby agrees to attend school each day from 10 to 2 and be ready to leave for school by 9:30 (dressed, hair combed, teeth brushed, and backpack with all homework).

Should he not complete his responsibility, he will be required to attend school "as is" and not allowed to attend football practice or play on Saturday.

In the event that all terms of the contract are honored from Monday 9:30 am to Friday 6:00 pm, Bobby will be transported to Blockbuster and allowed to rent any non-M game of his choice.

Bobby and his parents agree to uphold the conditions of the contract and read and initial it each night before going to bed and each morning before going to school.

_____
Signature   Date: _____

_____
Signature   Date: _____

_____
Signature   Date e: _____

Communication Skills Training

Kearney and Silverman (1995) reported that many of these children are from families where poor communication is a major issue. This will likely make contracting and negotiating a contract for school attendance very difficult. Initial efforts may focus on basic interactional problems such as, interrupting, poor listening, silence, refusal to communicate, and arguing. A family therapist or counselor can help establish communication rules during the negotiation of the contract: i.e. no insults, no sarcasm, volume, etc. It may be necessary to utilize mediation and negotiation techniques by initially working with various dyads and triads within the family to minimize conflict and establish a workable contract. Total effective family communication may become an issue for counseling once some level of agreement and trust has been reached.

Peer Refusal Training

Peer influence may be more motivating than any reinforcers that could be established in a school attendance contract. Many children may not be attending school as a result of being influenced by their peers to "ditch" or "cut" school. Peer refusal training is most useful for those who intend to stay in school, but succumb to pressure to leave early or to never arrive at school and meet their peers at some other location. The counselor can be effective by obtaining a description of what peers are saying or doing to entice non-attendance and providing the youth with rebuttal statements through modeling and role playing. Workable strategies to respond to peer pressure, without social ridicule or rejection, may reduce absences.

Chapter Eleven

Practical Strategies for School Personnel and Parents

Forced School Attendance

If a child is completely absent from school, missing for a significant portion of the time in a chronic fashion, and other attempts at producing a change in behavior have failed, it may be appropriate to begin thinking about ways to physically bring the child to school. Forced attendance is viewed as a "flooding" procedure with the goal of eventually creating habituation and a successful adaptation to attending school. Originating in the mid 60's Forced School Attendance was reported to be a very successful behavior modification technique. Kennedy (1965), in a limited sample study, reported 100% success for first episode of school refusal. While no technique is 100% successful, this technique has been replicated frequently enough to justify its efficaciousness.

Key to this approach is the concept of habituation, which can be acquired by gradual desensitization or by "flooding" the organism with the feared stimuli until habituation takes place. School personnel and parents are encouraged to "keep the child there" by whatever means necessary. While this is not a license to be physically or verbally abusive, it may be necessary to use safe physical management techniques. This technique requires an adult who ignore somatic complaints or disruptive behaviors, and simply require compliance with the directive to "sit in your desk." The technique requires a good working relationship between the parents and school personnel, as there may be a period of significant disruption to the classroom and acting out at home until the habituation takes place.

Forced School Attendance requires some caution with those children whose school refusal behavior is extremely anxiety based, i.e. children who are attempting to avoid stimuli which produce significant negative affect (SPNA) and those youth who are attempting to avoid the negative social and evaluative aspects of school attendance (EASE). In some instances, attempting to use this technique for youth whose school refusal behaviors are highly anxiety based (SPNA and EASE) may actually result in traumatizing the child and creating more significant and pathological resistance (Kearney and Albano, 2000).

Steps for Forced School Attendance (Kearney and Albano, 2007)

1. Parents prepare the child for school – physically, if necessary
2. Issue a command for the child to go to the car or bus "or we will take you"
3. If the child refuses, issue a warning
4. If refusal persists, parents physically carry the child to the car. One drives; one manages misbehavior in the back seat; no physical or emotional abuse.
5. Ignore inappropriate behavior, work through tantrums, and maintain a neutral demeanor
6. Upon arrival at school, issue the command to leave the car and go to school

114

7. If refusal persists, parents and school personnel physically take the child into the building.

Forced Attendance is most effective for those youth whose school refusal behavior is attention based (ASB). As a result of the potential for misuse of the Forced Attendance technique, Kearney and Albano (2000) developed guidelines for the use of Forced Attendance. Their guidelines indicate that this technique is only appropriate when:

- The child is refusing school the majority of the time and other interventions have been unsuccessful.
- The child is refusing school only for attention (AS) and has little distress or anxiety about attending school itself.
- Parents must be willing to take the child to school and school officials must be willing to meet the child at the door and serve as "escorts" and even supervise classroom behavior.
- Two parents or one parent and another trusted adult take the child to school to manage misbehavior (and then leave).
- The child is clear about the consequences of what happens if he or she refuses school.
- The child must be under 11 years of age.
- Parents and school personnel must be willing to expend the considerable effort which this technique requires.
- Parents and school personnel understand that some children are quite "strong willed" and the procedure may takes several days or even weeks. Parents must be warned in advance about the risk and danger of stopping the technique prematurely and the conditioning contingency that is established if the child is reinforced by getting his way for "outwitting and outlasting" the attempts of adults to make him compliant.

Escort Services

Escort Services is a process that is particularly effective with middle school children and high school aged youth who are refusing school to obtain other tangible rewards. The process of escort services is where a parent actually accompanies the child to school and remains with them for the entire day. The escort accompanies the child to school and to and from each class and for all school activities including lunch and other less structured activities such as gym and physical education. Understandably, this technique works best for a child seeking tangible reinforcers (TROS) and not with a child who is an attention seeker (ASB). Those children who are attention seekers may actually welcome the idea that their parent would accompany them to school. This is a technique that should never be used as a "bluff" or threat. Some children may be so oppositional that they will "call your bluff." Even those children who "call your bluff" typically cannot last more than one or two days with their parents attending school with them before they will acquiesce to attending school. In most situations, the credible threat of escorting and accompanying a child to school creates enough social apprehension to obtain school attendance (Kearney, 2001).

Escort Services requires the cooperation of school officials who are willing to have parents in their school in a "supervisory" capacity. Ideally the "escort" might be a non-parent, Aunt/Uncle, Grandparent, or the parent least emotionally involved with the child. Grandparents can be particularly effective as many of them have the time and commitment to the child to actually carry out the escorting services. In addition to the negative components to escorting the child, the child must have the ability to obtain rewards for attendance once their behavior is back under self-management.

Suggestions for Parents

Parents play a crucial role in the management and redirection of school refusal behaviors. It is important to have both parents actively involved even when custody is split or joint. Not allowing the child to triangulate parents around the issue of school refusal behavior can be the parents' most effective intervention. Specifically parents can:

- Believe that your child will get over the problem and let them know that you believe they can handle it.
- Listen to your child and encourage them to talk about their fears at times other than when you are attempting to obtain school attendance.
- Be understanding, use reflective listening don't use shame.
- Maintain good contact with school and teacher.
- Make sure that the child knows you will return to pick them up or that they are provided adequate supervision after school.
- Prepare them with gradual separations.
- Inform them that you expect them to stay for the entire day.
- Leave quickly (don't look back or hover).
- Do not reinforce the child's distress by rescuing
- Tell the child you will be doing something boring at home.
- Be reliable and on time when picking up your child.
- Have the other parent, a relative, a neighbor, or someone else who is less emotionally involved with the child take the child to school.

- Let the child have something of yours to keep in her pocket i.e. a symbol or picture.
- Give the child as much control as possible through providing them the illusion of control (Do you want to wear your green sweater or red shirt when you go to school today?).
- Prolonged goodbyes don't help the situation. A firm, caring, and quick separation is best for all concerned.

Suggestions for School Personnel

School personnel are in a unique position to create an environment for the child at school that will substantially increase the likelihood that the child will return and/or continue to attend school. School administrators, school counselors, and teachers can acquaint themselves with the dynamics of the school refusal and understand their component in the intervention plan. Specifically school personnel can:

- Connect the child with a teacher who understands the situation and matches the personality and learning style of the child. A 'goodness of fit" between a child who struggles with attendance and a teacher can be a significant factor in determining whether or not an intervention plan succeeds.
- Be particularly concerned about the child's homeroom teacher. If the first adult that a child will encounter at school is his favorite teacher, that connection may allow the child to overcome his resistance to getting to school.
- If possible, arrange for the school refuser to be in homeroom with as many of his friends as possible. While the child may have great anxiety about attending

school, being in the presence of his friends may help ease that anxiety.

- Provides as much insulation as possible from the bullies, insensitive, and tactless children.
- Customize the educational approach and curriculum to meet the child's needs
- Help the child identify "safe people" and "safe places" in the school or in the classroom that they can seek out when they are overwhelmed.
- Provide the student with easy access to counseling staff.
- Do not punish for late arrival at school, but rather reinforce the fact that they got to school and the courage that took.
- Have an arrival ritual where the child is met by a warm and supportive person.
- Encourage the student and parents to increase the amount of time that they are separated at home.
- Provide for testing and other high anxiety activities to be done in a separate location.
- Carefully match the student with other students for group activities or projects.
- Provide social skills training in a small group for children with similar struggles.
- Provide alternatives to reduce exposure to anxiety provoking situations (i.e. recording an oral report rather than presenting in front of the class.)
- Coach the child on coping strategies for anxiety provoking situations.
- Focus on relapse prevention strategies once the child returns to school, particularly in transitioning from one school year to the next.

School Refusal Bibliography

Achenbach, T.M. (1991). *Manual for the Child Behavior Checklist/4-18 and 1991 profile.* Burlington: University of Vermont, Department of Psychiatry.

Albano, A.M., Chorpita, B.F., & Barlow, D.H. (2003). Childhood anxiety disorders. In E. Marsh and R. Barkley (Eds.), *Child psychopathology (279-330).*New York, NY: The Guilford Press.

American Psychiatric Association: *Diagnostic and Statistical Manual of Mental Disorders,* Fourth Edition, Text Revision. Washington, DC, American Psychiatric Association, 2000.

Berg, I. (1996). School avoidance, school phobia, and truancy. In: M. Lewis (ed.), *Child and Adolescent Psychiatry.* Baltimore, MD: Williams and Wilkins.

Berg, I. (1997). School refusal and truancy. *Archives of Disease in Childhood, 76,* 90-91.

Bernstein, G.A., Burckhardt C.M., & Erwin, A.R. (2000). Imipramine plus cognitive-behavioral therapy in the treatment of school refusal. *Journal of the American Academy of Child and Adolescent Psychiatry, 39,* 276–283.

Bernstein, G.A., Helter, J.M. Burckhardt C.M., & McMillan, M.H. (2001). Treatment of school refusal: one-year follow-up. *Journal of the American Academy of Child and Adolescent Psychiatry, 40,*206–213.

Broadwin, I.T. (1932). A contribution to the study of Truancy. *American Journal of Orthopsychiatry, 2,* 253-259.

Chorpita, B.F., Albano, A.M., Holmberg, R.G., & Barlow, D.H. (1996). A systematic replication of the prescriptive treatment of school refusal behavior in a single subject. *Journal of Behavior Therapy and Experimental Psychiatry, 27 (3),* 281 – 290.

Chou, L.C., Ho, C.Y., Chen, C.Y. & Chen, W.J. (2006). Truancy and illicit drug use among adolescents surveyed via street outreach. *Addictive Behaviors, 31,* 149-154.

Coolidge, J.C., Hahn, P.B., & Peck, A.L. (1957). School Phobia: Neurotic crisis or way of life? *American Journal of Orthopsychiatry, 27,296-306.*

Costello, E.J., Egger, H., & Angold, A. (2005). 10 year research update review: The epidemiology of child and adolescent psychiatric disorders: Methods and public health burden. *Journal of the American Academy of Child and Adolescent Psychiatry, 44,* 972-986.

Dube, S.R. & Orpinas, P. (2009). Understanding excessive school absenteeism as school refusal behavior. *Children and Schools, 31(2)* 87-95.

Duckworth, K. & debug, J. (1989). Inhibiting class cutting among high school students. *High School Journal, 72,* 188-195.

Egger, H., Costello, E.J., & Angold, A. (2003). School refusal and psychiatric disorders: A community study. *Journal of the American Academy of Child and Adolescent Psychiatry, 42,* 797-807.

.

Evans, L.D. (2000). Functional School Refusal Subtypes: Anxiety, avoidance, and malingering. *Psychology in the Schools, Vol. 37(2),* 183-191.

Flakierska-Praquin, N., Lindstrom M., & Gill berg, C. (1997). School phobia with separation anxiety disorder: a comparative 20– to 29–year follow-up study of 35 school refusers. *Comparative Psychiatry.* 38:17–22.

Fremont, W. P. (2003). School refusal in children and adolescents. *American Family Physician, 68, 8,* 1555-1560.

Halfors, D., Cho, H., Brandish, P.H., Feeling, R. & Khatapoush, S. (2006). Identifying high school students "at risk" for substance use and other behavioral problems: Implications for prevention. *Substance Use and Misuse, 41,* 1-15.

Heyne, D. & Rollings, S. (2006) *School Refusal: Parent, Adolescent and Child Training Skills.* Oxford, UK: Blackwell Publishing.

Johnson, A.M., Falstein, E.T., Szurek, S.A., & Svenden, M. (1941). School phobia. *American Journal of Orthopsychiatry, 11,* 702-711.

Kearney, C.A. (2001). *School refusal behavior in youth: A functional approach to assessment and treatment.* Washington, DC: American Psychological Association.

Kearney, C.A. (2002a). Case study of the assessment and treatment of a youth with multifunction school refusal behavior. *Clinical Case Studies, 1,* 67-80.

Kearney, C.A. (2002b). Identifying the function of school refusal behavior: a revision of the School Refusal Assessment Scale. *Journal of Psychopathological Behavior Assessment, 24:* 235-245.

Kearney, C.A. (2005). *Social Anxiety and social phobia in youth: Characteristics, assessment, and treatment.* New York, NY: Springer.

Kearney, C.A. (2006a) Solutions to school refusal for parents and kids: Pinpoint and address reinforcers of the child's behavior. *Current Psychiatry, 5,* 67-83.

Kearney, C.A. (2006b). Dealing with school refusal behavior: A primer for family physicians. *The Journal of Family Practice, 55(8),* 51-71.

Kearney, C.A. (2007a). *Getting your child to say "yes" to school.* New York, NY: Oxford University Press.

Kearney, C.A. (2007b). Forms and functions of school refusal behavior in youth: An empirical analysis of absenteeism severity. *Journal of Child Psychology and Psychiatry, 48,* 53-61.

Kearney, C.A. (2008a). *Helping school refusing children and their parents: A guide for school-based professionals.* New York, NY: Oxford University Press.

Kearney, C.A. (2008b). School absenteeism and school refusal behavior: A review of contemporary literature. *Clinical Psychology Review, 28(3),* 451-471.

Kearney, C.A., & Albano, A.M. (2000). *When children refuse school: A cognitive –behavioral therapy approach – Therapists Guide.* San Antonio, TX: The Psychological Corporation.

Kearney, C.A., & Albano, A.M. (2007). *When children refuse school: A cognitive –behavioral therapy approach – Therapists Guide. Second Edition.* New York, NY: Oxford University Press.

Kearney, C.A., Pursell, C., & Alvarez, K (2001). Treatment of school refusal behavior in children with mixed functional profiles. *Cognitive and Behavioral Practice,8,* 3-11.

Kearney, C.A. & Silverman, W.K. (1990). A preliminary analysis of a functional model of assessment and treatment for school refusal behavior. *Behavior Modification, 14(3), 340-366..*

Kearney, C.A. & Silverman, W.K. (1995). Family environment of youngsters with school refusal behavior: A synopsis with implications for assessment and treatment. *American Journal of Family Therapy, 23(1),* 59-72.

Kearney, C.A. & Silverman, W.K. (1996). The evolution and reconciliation of taxonomic strategies for school refusal behavior. *Clinical Psychology: Science and Practice, 3(4),* 339-354.

Kearney, C.A. & Silverman, W.K. (1998). A critical review of pharmacotherapy for youth with anxiety disorders: Things are not as they seem. *Journal of Anxiety Disorders, 12,83-102.*

Kearney, C.A. & Silverman, W.K. (1999). Functionally based prescriptive and nonprescriptive treatment for children and adolescents with school refusal behavior. *Behavior Therapy, 30,* 673-695.

Kearney, C.A. & Silverman, W.K. (2002) Measuring the function of school refusal behavior; The School Assessment Scale. *Journal of Clinical Child Psychology, 22,* 85-96.

Kendall, P.C., Kane, M., Howard, B., & Siqueland, L.
(1992).*Cognitive Behavioral Therapy for Anxious Children: Therapist Manual.* Philadelphia: Workbook Publishing.

Kennedy, W.A. (1965). School phobia: Rapid treatment of fifty cases. *Journal of Abnormal Psychology, 70,* 285-289.

King, N.J. & Bernstein, G.A. (2001). School refusal in children and adolescents: A review of the past 10 years. *Journal of the American Academy of Child and Adolescent Psychiatry,40,* 197-205.

King, N.J., Ollendick, T.H., & Tonge, B.J. (1995). *School refusal: Assessment and treatment.* Needham Heights, MA: Allyn and Bacon.

King, N.J., Tonge, B.J., Heyne, D., & Ollendick, T.H. (2000). Research on the cognitive-behavioral treatment of school refusal: A review and recommendations. *Clinical Psychology Review, 20,* 495-507.

King, N.J., Tonge, B.J., Heyne, D., Pritchard, M., Rollings, S., Young, D., Meyerson, N. & Ollendick, T.H. (1998). Cognitive-behavioral treatment of school refusing children: A controlled evaluation. *Journal of the American Academy of Child and Adolescent Psychiatry, 37,* 395-403.

Kogan, S.M., Luo, Z., Murry, V.M., & Brody, G.H. (2005). Risk and protective factors for substance use among African-American high school dropouts. *Psychology of Addictive Behaviors, 19, 382-391.*

Last, C.G. & Strauss, C.C. (1990). School refusal in anxiety-disordered children and adolescents. *Journal of the American Academy of Child and Adolescent Psychiatry, 29,* 31-35.

Last, C.G., Hansen, C., & Franco, N. (1998). Cognitive-behavioral treatment of school phobia. *Journal of the American Academy of Child and Adolescent Psychiatry,37,* 404-411.

National Center for Education Statistics (2006). *The condition of education 2006.* Washington, DC: US Department of Education.

Ollendick, T.H. & Mayer, J.A. (1984). School phobia. In S.M. Turner (ed.) *Behavioral Theories and Treatment of Anxiety.* New York: Plenum (pp.36-411).

Seidel, L., & Walkup, J.T. (2006). Selective serotonin reuptake inhibitor use in the treatment of the pediatric non-obsessive-compulsive disorder anxiety diagnoses. *Journal of Child and Adolescent Psychopharmacology, 16,* 171-179.

Setzer, N. & Salzhauer, A. (2001). Understanding School Refusal. *NYU Child Study Center*

Silverman, W.K. & Kurtines, W.M. (1996). *Anxiety and phobic disorders: A pragmatic approach.* New York: Plenum Press.

Silverman, W. K., Pina, A. A., & Viswesvaran, Chockalingam (2008). Evidence-based psychosocial treatments for phobic and anxiety disorders in children and adolescents: A review and meta-analyses. *Journal of Clinical Child & Adolescent Psychology, 37,* 105-130.

Riddle, M.A., Bernstein, G.A., Cook, E.H., Leonard, H.L., March, J.S., & Swanson, J.M. (1999). Anxiolytics, adrenergic agents, and naltrexone. *Journal of the American Academy of Child and Adolescent Psychiatry, 38*:546–56.

Roebuck, M.C., French, M.T., & Hurrelmann, K. (1999). Adolescent marijuana use and school attendance. *Economics of Education Review, 23*, 133-141.

Terry, P.M. (1998). Do schools make students fearful and phobic? Focus: nurturing, caring relationships in today's schools. *Journal for a Just & Caring Education, 4*(2), 193-212.

Tyrrell, M. (2005). School phobia. *Journal of School Nursing, 21*, 147-151.

Wimmer, M.B. (2003). *School Refusal: Assessment and Interventions within school settings.* Bethesda, MD: National Association of School Psychologists.

Appendix A
Sample Case Study Responses

Eric Eggplant: School Makes Me Want to Throw Up

Type of School Refusal *Avoidance of Stimuli that Provoke Negative Affectivity*
Underlying or Comorbid Conditions *Generalized Anxiety Disorder, Parental Conflict, Dependency Issues, Specific Phobias, Enuresis*
Goal 1 *Decrease General Anxiety and Activation Levels*
    Objective 1 *Confront irrational fears and beliefs*
    Objective 2 *Provide instruction around relaxation techniques and self-talk*
    Objective 3 *Provide a set of specific coping strategies to use at school*
Goal 2 *Reduce Reactivity to School and Negative Affect Regarding School*
    Objective 1 *Establish an Affective/Avoidance Hierarchy*
    Objective 2 *Institute imaginal desensitization procedures*
    Objective 3 *Institute In-Vivo desensitization procedures*
Goal 3 *Determine the nature of physical symptoms*
    Objective 1 *Refer for physical examination to rule out organic basis*
Goal 4 *Increase school attendance and length of time at school*
    Objective 1 *Establish a reward contingency for school attendance*
    Objective 2 *Establish a consequence contingency for school refusal*

Nicholas Noodle: Everybody There Hates Me

Type of School Refusal *Escape from Aversive Social or Evaluative Situations*
Underlying or Comorbid Conditions *Social Phobia, Rule out Dysthymia*
Goal 1 *Identify social situations which produce anxiety*
    Objective 1 *Establish anxiety and avoidance hierarchy*
    Objective 2 *Determine anxiety "triggers"*
Goal 2 *Increase social skills and comfort in social settings*
    Objective 1 *Participate in a formal social skills group*
    Objective 2 *Challenge social misperceptions and increase communication skills*
    Objective 3 *Provide relaxation training and social skills role modeling*
    Objective 4 *Provide social support from other students through mentoring*
Goal 3 *Provide information regarding the nature of social anxiety*
    Objective 1 *Parents to participate in psychoeducation classes*
    Objective 2 *Educate the child regarding the nature of social anxiety*
Goal 4 *Challenge Cognitive Distortions about new school setting*
    Objective 1 *Reduce catastrophic thinking*
    Objective 2 *Increase positive self-talk*
    Objective 3 *Analyze the impact of all-or-none thinking patterns*

Rebecca Rigatoni: Can't I Stay Home and Have You Teach Me

Type of School Refusal *Attention Seeking Behaviors*
Underlying or Comorbid Conditions *Separation Anxiety, Rule Out Oppositional Defiant Disorder*
Goal 1 *Decrease Anxiety around separation issues*
    Objective 1 *Confront irrational fears and beliefs*
    Objective 2 *Provide instruction around relaxation techniques and self-talk*
    Objective 3 *Establish a symbolic connection with parent*
Goal 2 *Increase school attendance*
    Objective 1 *Establish a reward contingency for school attendance*
    Objective 2 *Establish a consequence contingency for school refusal*
    Objective 3 *Develop a standardized "morning routine" with predictability*
Goal 3 *Determine the nature of physical symptoms*
    Objective 1 *Refer for physical examination to rule out organic basis*
Goal 4 *Coordinate with school for consistent plan to address in class behavior*
    Objective 1 *Develop "allowance" plan for contacting mother during school hours*
    Objective 2 *Develop communication and feedback system for school and home*
    Objective 3 *Establish consequences to extinguish behavior*

School Refusal in Children and Adolescents Post-Test

Completion of this post-test ,at a level of 70% will entitle the reader to four continuing education credits. Complete the post-test and mail a copy, along with a $50.00 fee for CEU credits to:

Foundations: Education and Consultation
1400 B Browns Lane
Louisville, KY 40207

A certificate will be mailed in approximately 7 to 10 business days.

1. By birth order, the child most likely to have a significant issue with school refusal is:
    a. The only child
    b. The first born
    c. The middle child
    d. The last born.

2. Long term impacts of school refusal include all of the following **except**:
    a. Academic underachievement
    b. Autonomy issues,
    c. Early physical and emotional withdrawal from the family of origin.
    d. Higher risk for mental health issues as adults.

131

3. The truant child, as opposed to the child who is refusing school, is likely to:
   a. Complete all homework and make-up assignments
   b. Attempt to conceal their absence from parents
   c. Is likely to be someplace other than home during school hours
   d. Lacks excessive anxiety or fear about going to school

4. Kearney and Silverman defined the concept of school refusal to exclude those children who:
   a. Are absent from school for non-consecutive days
   b. Those who initially attend for part of the day and then leave
   c. Those arrive at school late after a behavioral incident
   d. Display unusual distress and plead to go home

5. School refusal is
   a. More frequently observed in boys than girls
   b. More frequently observed in girls than boys
   c. Equally common among boys and girls
   d. Only observed in minority children

6. Kearney and Silverman identify families of school refusers as exhibiting the following traits:
   a. Enmeshed, conflicted, detached, depressed, and healthy
   b. Enmeshed, conflicted, detached, isolated, and healthy
   c. Enmeshed, conflicted, detached, isolated, mixed, and healthy
   d. Enmeshed, pathological, detached, isolated, and healthy

7. The critical distinction between acute school refusal and chronic school refusal is based on
   a. Time absent from school.
   b. Time absent and the disruptive nature of the behavior
   c. The problem persists from one school year to the next
   d. The problem does not resolve itself spontaneously

8. School refusal can occur at all ages, but peaks at
   a. 5-7, 11, and 14
   b. 6 and 16
   c. 8 and 14
   d. 3, 14, and 16.

9. The categorical model of school refusal
   a. Does not lend itself to developing treatment programs
   b. Provides a common vocabulary across professions
   c. Is only concerned with the severity of behavior
   d. Is only interested in the motivation and purpose of behavior

10. Kearney's Functional Model of School Refusal
    a. Views all school refusal behavior as pursuing positive experiences
    b. Views all school refusal behavior as avoiding negative experiences.
    c. Views all school refusal behavior as either pursuing positive experiences or as avoiding negative experiences
    d. None of the above

11. Students who refuse school to avoid stimuli that produce general negative affect display
    a. Many delinquent and aggressive behaviors
    b. Many somatic symptoms and somatization
    c. Have highly pathological families
    d. Are not prone to various anxiety disorders

12. Students who refuse school to escape social or evaluative situations are
    a. Not likely to have experienced significant embarrassment, ridicule or rejection
    b. Are comfortable speaking before the class, writing on the board, and being in performance classes
    c. Score higher on measures of general anxiety, depression, and social anxiety
    d. Experience less social isolation in the community

13. Attention Seeking School Refusers tend to be
    a. Older than other school refusers
    b. Less likely to engage in tantrums, non-compliance, and running away
    c. Struggling with Separation Anxiety Disorder, Generalized Anxiety Disorder (GAD), and Oppositional Defiant Disorder
    d. From families with well established individual boundaries

14. School refusers who are not attending school in order to obtain tangible reinforcers
    a. Are less anxiety based and more a result of an inability to delay gratification
    b. Have higher levels of distress about going to school
    c. Show high levels of communication between family members
    d. None of the above

15. Which of the following is not frequently comorbid with school refusal
    a. Separation Anxiety
    b. Generalized Anxiety
    c. Post Traumatic Stress Disorder
    d. Panic Attacks

16. Which of the following is part of the diagnostic criteria for Attention Deficit Hyperactivity Disorder
    a. Symptoms must have occurred prior to age seven
    b. Symptoms must be present in two or more settings
    c. Both A and B
    d. None of the above

17. A thorough assessment of school refusers will likely include a review all of the following except:
    a. A complete medical history
    b. Consideration of other Axis I disorders
    c. A joint interview with the child and parent(s)
    d. The presence of Anxiety and/or Depression

18. Developing a standard assessment approach for school refusers should
    a. Rely solely on standardized test
    b. Rely in some part on collateral information
    c. Not attempt to identify levels of anxiety and depression
    d. All the above

19. Children who are willfully disobedient and refuse to attend school should be diagnosed as having
    a. Conduct Disorder
    b. Major Depressive Disorder
    c. Panic Attacks
    d. Oppositional Defiant
    e. None of the above

20. Which of the following is **not** a true statement:
    a. Adolescents and even very young children can be diagnosed with Obsessive Compulsive Disorder if they have sufficient symptoms.
    b. Panic Disorder and Panic Attacks are frequently observed in elementary and middle school children
    c. Diagnostic criteria for a Major Depressive Episode are not exactly the same for children and adults.
    d. Oppositional Defiant Disorder is frequently observed in children from families with marital discord, substance abuse, and depression.

21. An approach to school refusal that has been demonstrated to be 83 percent successful is:
    a. Dialectical Behavior Therapy
    b. Pharmacological Intervention
    c. Cognitive Behavior Therapy
    d. None of the above

22. Which of the following is a true statement:
    a. Benzodiazepines are not recommended for use with children or adolescents due to danger of dependence, withdrawal, and drug tolerance
    b. It has been conclusively demonstrated that there is no increased suicide risk using SSRI's with children and adolescents.
    c. Using SSRI's with children who have a family history of Bipolar Disorder is typically very effective
    d. None of the above

23. Family therapy with school refusal behavior might focus on all these aspects of family functioning except:
    a. The family messages
    b. Reinforcement contingencies
    c. Rewarding dysfunctional behavior.
    d. Identifying the pathology of the school refuser

24. Which of the following strategies are appropriate for those youth who engage in school refusal behaviors to escape the social and evaluative aspects of school attendance
    a. Role play
    b. Cognitive restructuring of negative self-talk
    c. Social skills training and reduction of social anxiety
    d. All of the above
    e. None of the above

25. All **but** the following are legitimate cognitive/behavioral strategies for working with a child whose school refusal is motivated by avoidance of stimuli that produce negative affect:
   a. Clarifying unreasonable or unrealistic expectations about school
   b. Psychotropic medications
   c. Systematic Desensitization
   d. Somatic control exercises

26. Assisting a child in establishing an Affective-Avoidance hierarchy is very effective for a child whose school refusal is motivated by avoidance of stimuli that produce negative affect because:
   a. It allows the child to compartmentalize aspects of the problem in terms of intensity
   b. The process assists the child in understanding the difference between a "fear" and an activity which does not produce a fear response, but one which is undesirable.
   c. Concrete behavioral objectives can be established to complete some of the undesirable or avoidance behaviors
   d. All the above

27. Youth who refuse to attend school to escape aversive social or evaluative situations typically may have
   a. Had limited success in social interactions in the past at school
   b. View themselves as shy, awkward, and different
   c. Either under communicate or over communicate
   d. Misinterpret social cues
   e. All the above

28. Cognitive Restructuring may lead a child with social avoidance issues to
    a. Catastrophize about social situations
    b. Create self-fulfilling prophesies
    c. Lead to poorer social performance due to over thinking
    d. Allow a child to experience their cognitions and feelings in a more productive and fruitful fashion

29. Which of the following may **not** be a particularly effective strategy working with a child whose school refusal is motivated by attention seeking:
    a. Restructuring Parent Commands
    b. Role playing activities
    c. Ignoring inappropriate behaviors
    d. Not responding to excessive requests for reassurance

30. The components of functionally based treatment for school refusers who are seeking tangible rewards for not attending school may include:
    a. Contracting for school attendance
    b. Escorting the child to school
    c. Communication skills training
    d. Peer refusal skills training
    e. All of the above

31. Forced Attendance is a rapid treatment procedure that
    a. Focuses on the nature of physical symptoms
    b. Requires the child to attend "by any means necessary"
    c. Is viewed as a "flooding procedure"
    d. A and B
    e. B and C

32. Forced Attendance has been demonstrated to work most effectively with school refusers who
    a. Are attempting to avoid stimuli that produce negative affect
    b. Are attempting to avoid the social and evaluative aspects of school attendance
    c. Are refusing school as a means of gaining attention
    d. Are Refusing school to obtain tangible rewards

33. Which of the following is **not** a true statement about intervening with school refusers who are attention seekers:
    a. Calls home to seek reassurance should be placed on a diminishing reinforcement schedule.
    b. Treatment/intervention for a child who refuses to attend school for attention does not require working to change parenting styles.
    c. Lecturing, yelling, negotiating, trying to be calm, or physical force work does not generally work with school refusers who are attention seekers.
    d. The focus of the intervention will be primarily with the parents making changes

34. Which of the following strategies will be most effective with school refusers who are seeking tangible rewards for their school refusal
    a. Developing an attendance contract
    b. Working to improve communication between the parents and child
    c. Empowering the child with peer refusal strategies
    d. All of the above

35. Using a Forced Attendance strategy to deal with school refusal is typically only appropriate for :
    a. A child who is refusing school a majority of the time
    b. A child who has little distress or anxiety about attending school
    c. A child who is under the age of 11
    d. A child whose parents are fully committed to the technique and willing to expend considerable effort
    e. All of the above

I_____, the **undersigned attest to the fact that I read the materials and am the person who completed the post test.**

_____

Signature   **Date**

Mail CEU certificate to:

_____

Name

_____

Address

_____

City, State, Zip Code